ADVENTURE RACING

ADVENTURE RACING

THE ULTIMATE GUIDE

LIZ CALDWELL
BARRY SIFF

FOREWORD BY
IAN ADAMSON

VELO
press®

Boulder, Colorado USA

Printed in the United States of America
Distributed in the United States and Canada by Publishers Group West
International Standard Book Number: 1-884737-90-0

Library of Congress Cataloging-in-Publication Data
Caldwell, Liz.
      Adventure racing : the ultimate guide / Liz Caldwell and Barry Siff.
              p. cm.
      Includes index.
      ISBN 1-884737-90-0
      1. Adventure racing—Handbooks, manuals, etc. I. Siff, Barry. II. Title.

      GV1038.S54 2001
      796.5—dc21   00-069256

Disclaimer: The publisher, editors, and authors shall not be held responsible for any injuries resulting from the use or misuse of information contained in this book.

Cover photos by Dan Campbell; © Dan Campbell
Photography in Park City, Utah; DANCAMPBELLPHOTOGRAPHY.COM.
Inline skating photo by Thomas Zuccareno; © 2000 Salomon N.A./Thomas Zuccareno.

Cover and interior design by Ann W. Douden

VeloPress
1830 North 55th Street
Boulder, Colorado 80301-2700 USA
303/440-0601 • FAX 303/444-6788 • E-MAIL velopress@7dogs.com

To purchase additional copies of this book or other VeloPress books, call 800/234-8356 or visit us on the Web at www.velopress.com.

To Gary, whose loving support makes it easy for me to chase my dreams. And to my son, Skylar, for making each day an adventure.

—LC

To Judy, Brian, and Elliot for your unwavering support and encouragement, and for putting up with me through the years. To Mom, for always giving me the freedom to do what I wanted, and to Toy Soldiers, for introducing me to the spectacular world of adventure racing.

—BS

CONTENTS

FOREWORD

One of my earliest impressions of Liz Caldwell and Barry Siff was during a snowy Colorado raft trip on the flooded Poudre River in the spring of 1999. Our raft was careening around in a rapid called "Death by Fish" or some other improbable name when suddenly Barry went overboard. Liz had her paddle poised and eyes alert in case Barry surfaced in her immediate vicinity, whilst I ambitiously poked an unlikely looking piece of flotsam on my side of the raft. After a sufficiently worrying period of time, Barry's red and bulging face exploded from the water and he executed an impressive breach towards the boat. Expecting at least a few words of dissent given the frigid conditions, I was pleasantly surprised to hear Barry exclaim, "Hair wsss ussss anasic!" My years of experience paddling cold rivers led me to understand he meant, "That was just fantastic!"

Embracing such an adventurous aquatic outing with high spirits and humor is a hallmark of good adventure athletes, and it left me with a very favorable impression of my hosts. As it turned out, our morning exercise was not only an exciting raft trip, it was a serious business meeting of the MountainQuest Adventures kind. Most of Liz and Barry's ideas, planning sessions, and meetings are conducted while actually doing something active, and it was my good fortune to be party to this particular "meeting."

I have subsequently been fortunate enough to be part of many successive meetings with Barry and Liz—running the spectacular trails behind Horsetooth Reservoir in Fort Collins, Colorado; mountain biking the Colorado Trail near Fruita, Colorado; and kayaking our local lakes. The reason I say fortunate is that Liz and Barry have a passion for adventure racing that surrounds them and infects everyone in their vicinity.

I have helped out at their MountainQuest camps and competed in their MountainQuest races, and found every single event efficient, well run, and eminently enjoyable. Although Liz and Barry have competed at a world-class level in many sports and have raced in all the major international adventure races, they embrace racers of all levels, from the casual weekend adventurer to serious athletes.

This book is a compilation of Liz and Barry's combined experience and knowledge, but it represents more than just great information and instructions. Between these covers you will find an energy representing their deep passion for the sport.

For anyone interested in delving into adventure racing for the first time, athletes crossing over from other sports, or anyone simply interested in what exactly adventure racers are up to while the rest of us sip our first coffee of the day, the following pages provide the insight, expertise, and information you are looking for.

IAN ADAMSON
Winner of the Eco-Challenge 2000 and
the Raid Gauloises 1998

PREFACE

Adventure racers come in many shapes and sizes, both young and old, from cities and villages all over the world. They are outdoors enthusiasts and athletes—runners, triathletes, hikers, paddlers, and adventurers. They are lawyers, doctors, educators, retirees, students, mothers, and fathers. What is it that draws such an eclectic group into this unique sport?

The spirit of the outdoors. The challenge. Seeing beautiful lands in an exploratory, unparalleled way. The team aspect. The variety of the disciplines. Learning new skills. The fun, the competition, and the thrill.

In the United States, most people interested in entering the sport of adventure racing have been turned on first by seeing or hearing about the Eco-Challenge®: The Expedition Race.™ Although not the first adventure race, the Eco-Challenge has become the most visible adventure race, particularly in the United States. Every year since 1995, the Eco-Challenge has been televised worldwide in an exciting multi-hour series. People everywhere have watched with curiosity and awe as coed teams of four compete around the clock for seven to ten days—battling nature and the elements, fatigue, and sometimes even themselves in a variety of sports including trekking, mountain biking, paddling, and mountaineering. The extraordinary images of racers rappelling through picturesque waterfalls, paddling through breathtaking whitewater, trekking over high mountains, or riding indigenous animals are certain to jumpstart the adrenaline flow of any outdoor enthusiast or multisport athlete.

© 2000 Don Gabrielson

Even with all of the diverse backgrounds and differing motivations of people wanting to do an adventure race, the question is nearly always the same: How does one get started? Camps such as MountainQuest Adventure Racing and Colorado Adventure Training have been a springboard for hundreds of people interested in learning how to get started in adventure racing. A large number have then gone on to become highly successful racers.

Over the years we have had the privilege of teaching many people about adventure racing. The information we have gained from teaching at our MountainQuest camps combined with what we have learned from competing successfully in races such as the Raid Gauloises and Eco-Challenge provides the foundation for this book.

There are various reasons to compete in adventure racing: for the personal challenge, to win, or for the wonderful sense of accomplishment that comes from completing the race. For many, the goal as a team is to remain friends, stay safe, and do the best that you can. Whatever your reasons and goals, this book will help you on your way.

Your first adventure race is exciting, as are all of the races that are bound to follow. The objective of this book is to get newcomers to the starting line of an adventure race armed with knowledge of the sport and confidence in their ability to achieve their goals. The most common questions that we are asked by newcomers as well as those interested in trying a longer race are answered in this book. Our aim is to help you learn the basics of adventure racing and discover what it takes to successfully compete in and complete an adventure race.

QUESTIONS MOST OFTEN ASKED ABOUT ADVENTURE RACING

- ▲ How do I get started?
- ▲ What do I wear on my feet while racing?
- ▲ What clothes should I wear during the race?
- ▲ What do I eat during a race?
- ▲ How do I find/select teammates?
- ▲ How should I train for an adventure race?
- ▲ Should I practice sleep deprivation?

ACKNOWLEDGMENTS

This book is an outgrowth of our passion for the sport of adventure racing and our desire to share our enthusiasm with as many people as possible. Our love of adventure racing is fueled by our interactions with many wonderful people, from friends and fellow athletes to sponsors.

First, and foremost, Ian Adamson has inspired us as a racer, teacher, and friend. The encouragement he gives us in our business, camps, and racing endeavors is unparalleled. He is an inspiration to many.

Several people have helped us throughout the years with our MountainQuest adventure race camps and races; most notably David Hake, Vicki Steele, Toby Wright, Steve Carr, Shawn Brooks, and Cindy Russell. Their love of everything outdoors inspires us as well as everyone attending our camps.

We are grateful to the thirteen brave souls who competed in the first MountainQuest race and have stuck with us ever since. And none of our races would have been as successful as they were without the dedication and expertise of Al Acker and the Grand Junction Hams and the many search and rescue organizations that have helped throughout the years.

We've been fortunate to have the support of numerous sponsors: Susie and Shannon and Jogmate; Liz Wilson and SportHill; Outlast Technologies; Uptime; HardCorps; New Belgium Brewing Company; and Princeton Tec. In addition, Laura Fogarty of Friction Free Technologies, Lawrence Motola at Adidas, and Bryan Johnston and the entire team at Salomon North America have been tremendous to work with. A very special thanks is due Emily Hahn at the Salomon Design Center for believing in us from the start.

Many of our adventure racing friends provided their personal training plans for Appendix B, including Ian Adamson, Mats Andersson, Robyn Benincasa, Antonio de la Rosa, Petri Forsman, Michael Kloser, Terho Lahtinen, Paul Romero, Rebecca Rusch, and Harald Zundel. We appreciate their dedication to the sport and willingness to share their knowledge.

We're grateful to Dan Campbell for providing many exciting adventure racing photos for this book (and for the rice and colas in Borneo!). We also acknowledge Darrin Eisman for his support, race coverage, and great photos over the years.

Thanks goes to Jill Redding for doing a wonderful job reviewing the original manuscript and making content suggestions, as well as continually supporting our efforts as racers and race directors through *Inside Triathlon*. We especially appreciate the enthusiasm and encouragement shown by Amy Sorrells and Theresa van Zante of VeloPress in helping us realize our goal of publishing this book.

Lastly, a special thanks to our adventure racing teammates who have pulled, pushed, and sung with us through many races, adding to our love and passion for the great sport of adventure racing.

INTRODUCTION

THE APPEAL OF ADVENTURE RACING

© 1998 Dan Campbell

What has made adventure racing such a dynamic and fast-growing sport worldwide? What has attracted young people in their twenties to compete alongside teammates old enough to be their parents? There are many answers to these questions, but the truth is that nearly every individual has a unique reason and motivation to become an adventure racer.

The sport began with a cadre of eclectic individuals who loved the outdoors and exploration, and, yes, they were a bit driven and competitive, too. They would climb mountains, cycle or ski to the bottom, kayak a bit, and then down a few beers together when it was all over. It was fun, exhilarating, and competitive—all while doing what they loved in the outdoors. Today, this type of camaraderie and friendly competition still attracts many people to adventure racing.

For some, adventure racing is the chance to learn new sports and develop new skills. If it weren't for adventure racing, the two of us may never have learned to scuba dive (for the Eco-Challenge 2000) or had the opportunity to "hydro-speed" (whitewater swim) for the Raid Gauloises 2000. Many adventure racers have learned to kayak, ascend and descend ropes, and navigate using a map and compass since becoming involved in the sport. Others, such as those with a military background, enjoy the sport because they can continue using some of the skills they learned while in the service.

Triathletes, endurance runners, and others are seeking "the next thing": the activity that will test their abilities, their mental as well as their physical strengths, and keep them active in something new, exciting, and cutting edge. A number of these individuals have helped take the sport from an "expedition" mindset to a more competitive one, creating a demand for shorter, faster adventure races, while pushing the limits of physical ability in the longer races.

© 2000 Dan Campbell

For many, doing an adventure race provides a challenge that is not only physical but mental as well. Adventure races contain three interrelated components: (1) the race itself—the competition, race course, format, and exploration of new areas, new cultures, and nature; (2) the team—both intra- and inter-team dynamics; and (3) the individual—the self and the ego. All three related components provide an opportunity, each time you race, to learn something new about your surroundings, either in foreign lands or your own backyard, to work together with others to reach a goal, and to stretch your perceived limits beyond what you thought possible—to discover that you can do more than you thought you could. A number of top competitors have referred to adventure races as a microcosm of life—pretty heady stuff, but certainly an appealing aspect of the sport to many racers. Some competitors describe the race experience as one in which the body is finally broken down enough to begin to discover our universal connectedness and true existence as "more than just a body," namely, the beginning of the letting go of ego.

The beauty of adventure racing is that there is plenty of room for all competitors with different backgrounds and athletic abilities—those who are still seeking the beauty and thrill of pure exploration while pushing their bodies physically, as well as those seeking good competition. The Salomon X-Adventure Race, a successful European race series held in seven different countries, came to the United States for the first time in 2000. The race featured world-class teams racing to win alongside many beginner teams whose goal was just to finish and have fun. Adventure racing allows each level of team, from the most experienced and competitive to the beginner, to have the experience they want.

Adventure races take place throughout the world. The opportunity to travel to new destinations is another appealing aspect of the sport. Top adventure races in 2000 were set in such exotic locations as Tibet, Nepal, Borneo, New Zealand, Brazil, and China. The perspective you gain for a country, its land, and its people is unique as you race through on foot, by bicycle, or on water. Traversing the countryside unlike an ordinary tourist, going through jungles or caves few people ever see, and interacting with the local people as you pass through their villages gives the adventure racer a view like no other. Even doing an adventure race in an urban area, such as downtown Chicago, or in a familiar place, like a state park near your hometown, allows racers to see the area in a new way—perhaps, in a more "primitive" or unencumbered way.

Historically, many of the top competitors in adventure racing have been in their late thirties and early to mid-forties. This is certainly appealing to lots of us "older folks." Maturity, experience, and skill in interpersonal relationships combined with a base of endurance goes a long way in adventure racing. Much of what is sought and gained by participating in an adventure race is also not always predicated upon speed or winning. It is often the experience, the achievement of a goal, or just doing something fun with friends.

For many, the team aspect of adventure racing is one of the most appealing features of the sport. The opportunities and challenges that each team member might face during an adventure race help that person to grow and better understand him- or herself. Sometimes you might be the team member in need of support, whereas at other times you will be the supportive team member. Traveling with a team through a race allows you to see others in a novel setting; you will observe how they respond to different situations and challenges, and see emotions, including your own, that otherwise might be kept hidden or rarely felt or seen. All of this adds up to an incredible journey of self-discovery while doing something you love.

Whether it's acquiring new skills, exploring new lands, discovering more about yourself, or just doing something that looks fun and exciting, adventure racing has a broad appeal and offers something unique to each of its participants.

PART ONE

THE
SPORT
OF
ADVENTURE
RACING

© 1996 Dan Campbell

CHAPTER 1

A BRIEF HISTORY OF MULTISPORT RACING

© 1995 Dan Campbell

In the beginning, there was New Zealand. There still is. The spirit and roots of adventure racing are embodied in the Kiwis of this tiny and rugged country. Although most Americans first became aware of adventure racing with the advent of the Eco-Challenge race in Utah in 1995, the Kiwis had already been "adventure racing" for twenty-plus years. Steve Gurney, a New Zealander and one of the most accomplished participants in the sport, was competing in long, crazy multisport races in his homeland in the mid-1970s: "I remember trekking up mountains, skiing down, and then paddling for hours and getting a beer for the accomplishment. It was good fun," he said. The roots of organized adventure racing stem from the first organized endurance multisport races, the Coast to Coast, started in New Zealand in 1980, and the Alaska Wilderness Classic held in Alaska since 1983.

RAID GAULOISES, SOUTHERN TRAVERSE, AND ECO-CHALLENGE

The Raid Gauloises, considered by most as the first official adventure race, was founded by Gerard Fusil of France in 1989. Fusil was a visionary. He wished to combine a myriad of nonmotorized modes of travel with an exploration of some of the most remote and beautiful lands in the world. Fittingly, he chose New Zealand as the site of the first Raid Gauloises. Fusil uniquely designed his race to be a team effort. Each team was composed of five people, with a requirement to have at least one female on the team. Teams were to compete as one, with all members staying together and successfully performing all segments of the race in order to be considered official finishers.

The Raid Gauloises was, and still is, a ten-day event for teams of five, and includes at a minimum the athletic disciplines of trekking, mountain biking, paddling, rope skills, and the art of navigation by map and compass. The race was immediately personified by the lack of a set course or marked trail; rather, teams were required to use their maps and a compass to select the best route to travel through the race. In the first years of existence, the Raid Gauloises popularized the new sport of adventure racing in Europe, Australia, and New Zealand.

Since its beginning the Raid Gauloises has taken place in:

New Zealand, 1989

Costa Rica, 1990

New Caledonia, 1991

Gulf of Oman, 1992

Madagascar, 1993

Malaysia, 1994

Argentina, 1995

Lesotho, 1997

Ecuador, 1998

Tibet/Nepal, 2000

Following the success of the Raid Gauloises, Geoff Hunt, an accomplished adventure racer and Raid Gauloises veteran, started the Southern Traverse Adventure Race in 1991. The Southern Traverse is held annually in New Zealand and is widely recognized the world over as one of the most difficult and navigationally challenging adventure races. During the first ten years the race was held, the Southern Traverse didn't receive much recognition from the general public outside of New Zealand, but recognition by racers as one of the "premier" adventure races in the world is growing. The Southern Traverse has historically been a shorter race than the Raid Gauloises, with the winning teams finishing in three to five days.

Mark Burnett, an entrepreneur living in southern California, heard of the Raid Gauloises and fielded a U.S. team in the race in 1992 in Oman and returned again to race in 1993. He was enamored with the idea of adventure racing and decided to produce his own adventure race, which he called the Eco-Challenge. Since its 1995 debut in the United States in Utah, the race has been held in British Columbia, Canada (1996), Australia (1997), Morocco (1998), Argentina (1999), and Borneo, Malaysia (2000).

Burnett altered the Raid Gauloises team format to teams of four of mixed gender. No all-female teams were allowed as they were in the Raid Gauloises. The uniqueness of this require-ment was that all competitors, whether female or male, would be competing on the same play-ing field.

Mark Burnett, executive director of Eco-Challenge: The Expedition Race.
© 2000 Dan Campbell

The sport of adventure racing was turbocharged by the advent of the Eco-Challenge in the United States. The first adventure race to have major television coverage each year, the Eco-Challenge became recognizable to the general public (particularly in the United States) and quickly became one of the premier adventure races in the sport. Mark Burnett has, arguably, done more for the growth and recogni-tion of adventure racing than anyone else in the world. He brought adventure racing successfully to the media and into your living room, and made it larger than life. Every year millions of people watch the Eco-Challenge on television, and so Mark Burnett, perhaps, did for adventure racing what Julie Moss did for the Hawaii Ironman Triathlon, in her famous crawl to the finish line in 1982—he has helped to make adventure racing a recognizable sport.

All three of the early adventure races (Raid Gauloises, Southern Traverse, and Eco-Challenge) encompassed five to ten days of racing in faraway foreign lands, and the expense and time required to compete in these races seemed beyond the reach of most athletes. As a result, a need for more achievable "shorter" adventure races was recognized, and races of several hours to one and two days were created. The Eco-Challenge staged two shorter races of twenty-four hours—Maine in 1995 and California in 1997—with the California race serving as a "qualifier" for the hugely popular longer Eco-Challenge.

ENTRY-LEVEL AND NEW ADVENTURE RACES

Recognizing the need for shorter adventure races, Michael Epstein, a successful sports promoter from California, started producing the Hi-Tec Adventure Racing Series in 1997. Hi-Tec races challenge coed teams of three for three to six hours of fun by combining trail running, mountain biking, paddling, and a series of special team "mystery events." Many adventure racing purists challenge the Hi-Tec races being called adventure races. Yet it is clear that the Hi-Tec racing series has provided a broad welcome mat to thousands of outdoor, multisport enthusiasts—providing an introduction to the adventure racing concept. In fact, more people have participated in the Hi-Tec Adventure Racing Series in the first three to four years of existence than both the Eco-Challenge and Raid Gauloises combined.

Other entry-level adventure races have sprung up all over the United States and internationally in the past several years. One- and two-day races of eight to thirty hours can be found nearly every weekend during the late spring to early fall months. Most of these races encompass the themes of team, mixed-gender, and multisport, nonmotorized activities. However, due to the cries of many who have found the challenge of putting a team together too daunting, as well as those seeking a more personal, individual challenge, an increasing number of races are allowing "solo" competitors. Additionally, teams of the same gender are being accepted into more and more events. Although these variations are a clear departure from the initial spirit of adventure racing, they have eased the entry for many into the sport and, thus, its growth overall. Many races, including both the Raid Gauloises and Eco-Challenge have held to their original team and gender requirements.

Newer and growing trends for the sport of adventure racing include more stage adventure races, where competitors race on consecutive days and stop at night, more shorter races and race series, and winter adventure races. No matter how one views the origin or official beginning of adventure racing, it remains a very young sport. The basic disciplines have remained—trekking, mountain biking, paddling, rope skills, and navigation—yet new and novel additions are found routinely, such as swimming, horse riding, inline skating, and caving, to name a few.

The Raid Gauloises, Southern Traverse and Eco-Challenge continue to be at the forefront of multiday adventure racing in terms of challenge and competition. However, more recently developed long races, such as the Mild Seven Outdoor Quest (a multiday staged event), the ELF Authentic Adventure (begun in 1999 by Gerard Fusil, now separated from the Raid he founded), the Beast of the East in the eastern United States, the Expedition Mata Atlantica (EMA) in Brazil, the Raid Aventura in Argentina, and others like them, will continue to grow over the years. These existing races will be joined by many other new races of varying length and difficulty that will help to enrich the sport of adventure racing and provide the opportunity to race to anyone who wants to.

CHAPTER 2

RACE STRUCTURE

© 1996 Dan Campbell

The classic definition of an adventure race is a self-supported, multiday, multisport team race, with a wilderness aspect. These races are generally non-stop, meaning that once the clock starts, the race continues until the first team crosses the finish line. Races were originally designed for coed teams of three to five people to complete together, staying together at all times, hence the popular adventure racing saying, "You are only as fast as your slowest team member." More recently, the definition of adventure racing has expanded to include any multisport race with a team component (and some-times solo competitors), regardless of the length of the race. The idea can be further categorized as follows:

- ▲ Sprint races—winning times are from two to eight hours and can include team categories and solo categories; example: Hi-Tec Adventure Racing Series.
- ▲ Weekend—winning times are twelve to thirty hours and cover 50 to 150 miles of terrain. Examples: MountainQuest Adventure Races, Raid the North Adventure Races, FogDog 24-Hour Adventure Race.
- ▲ Expedition-style races—the winners take from three to ten-plus days to complete the race, and the length of the race is from 250 to 500 miles. Examples: Raid Gauloises, Eco-Challenge, Southern Traverse, ELF Authentic Adventure Race.
- ▲ Stage races—two to four-day (or longer) races where the clock stops each day after a specified distance has been covered. The race

begins again the next day, and the winning team has the lowest cumulative time. Examples: Mild Seven Outdoor Quest, Salomon X-Adventure Race series, Salomon Winter Adventure Race.

The percentage of teams finishing the twenty-four-hour-plus races is often less than 50 percent. To give the less elite teams a chance to participate in and finish these races, weekend and expedition-length races are often further subdivided into different race categories. The ELF provides an Extreme, Adventure, and Discovery category that teams can select from. Teams that do not make certain race cutoffs that are set up along the course are not disqualified; they are simply moved into the next category and their course is shortened.

Races can be classified as "supported" or "nonsupported" events. A supported event means that each team has a support crew of one or two people and a vehicle that will transport the team's gear along the racecourse. The short, sprint adventure races are usually set up with a single transition so that there is no need to have team support personnel. Unsupported races are those, such as the Eco-Challenge and the ELF, that do no allow support teams; instead, race personnel transport all competitor gear to each transition area (TA). By doing this, both the Eco-Challenge and the ELF expand the expedition element so that the planning and organization of the race becomes a central part of each team's responsibility.

The number of teams allowed to compete in an adventure race varies and is often dictated by the race director. A maximum number of teams are often stipulated for safety reasons. The Raid Gauloises, Eco-Challenge, and Southern Traverse will have as many as seventy to eighty teams competing, whereas sprint adventure races such as the Hi-Tec Adventure Racing Series can have more than 250 teams competing in one race.

Most races are set up on a first-come, first-served registration basis; however, some, like the Eco-Challenge and the Mild Seven Outdoor Quest, have in the past required teams to submit detailed applications, which are then reviewed, and teams are selected to compete based on the submitted applications. The criteria for selection often go far beyond athletic ability and can include the "interest" factor of the team for media attention. Sometimes the battle for a spot in some of the popular races is even more competitive than the race itself. For example, in response to requests from many adventure racers, the Eco-Challenge changed its competitor selection process and opened the application for the 2000 and 2001 races to all potential competitors. In the United States, applications were accepted at 10 a.m. Pacific Time on one morning only—and only the first thirty-five applications were to be accepted. In less than two minutes, several hundred to one thousand applications were received, and as a result, a lottery was used to select teams from the United States. Several additional media-interest teams were selected from submitted applications to complete the total number of teams allowed to compete in the Eco-Challenge. Many races, from weekend to multiday races, sell out very quickly.

The entry fees for adventure races vary depending on the race location, team size, and length of race. Well-sponsored races often have more reasonable entry fees because the sponsorship money is picking up some of the cost that is usually born by the racers. Sprint adventure races can cost as little as $150 to $250 per three-person team. Weekend races can vary from $300 for a three-person team up to $1,000 or more for a four-person team. Expedition-style races often have entry fees as high as $7,500 to more than $13,000, plus the added expense of travel and accommodations. The time commitment (beyond training) for adventure races can be huge. To compete in the Raid Gauloises 2000, competitors had to be away from their homes for more than three weeks, and many of the top teams arrived at the race site even earlier to spend time acclimatizing. Even the weekend races can require that teams check in on Friday afternoon, before the race, so competitors may be required to take at least one day off from work to compete.

THE COST OF RACING

In 2000 the entry fee for U.S. competitors in the Raid Gauloises was $10,000. Additional fees included mandatory insurance packages, travel to a mandatory training and testing weekend in the United States prior to the race, a charter flight from Nepal to the race start in Tibet, and an accommodations package. As a result, it cost many seven-person teams (five racers plus two support members) about $50,000 to compete in the Raid Gauloises (not including required gear!).

RACE DISCIPLINES
OR SPORTS

An adventure race generally involves a variety of nonmotorized sports including, at a minimum, mountain biking, paddling (rafting, canoeing, kayaking), trekking, mountaineering (generally rope skills), and navigation or orienteering.

Sprint races include the core events of mountain biking, trail running, and paddling. In longer races, additional sports may be included, such as horseback riding, caving, canyoneering, and whitewater swimming. The Eco-Challenge attempts to incorporate the use of indigenous watercraft and sports or activities unique to an area into each of its races. The Raid Gauloises has been known to include new or exotic sports such as white (or wild) water swimming and even skydiving.

Crossing the mud pit in a Hi-Tec Adventure Racing Series race.
© Nathan Bilow

Many of the shorter adventure races, particularly the Hi-Tec racing series, have introduced "mystery events" or "special tests" into adventure racing. These generally take the form of team-building exercises or special tests designed to make the team members work together to find a solution to a problem. Examples include: greased wall climbs, cargo net climbs, log or hay bale carries, and jigsaw puzzles.

At the start of the Mild Seven Outdoor Quest 2000 held near Lijiang, Yunnan Province, China, competitors were given two buckets with holes punched in them, several sticks of chewing gum, a long piece of rope, and a Ping-Pong ball. The trick was to figure out how to fill one bucket containing the Ping-Pong ball with water from a nearby stream so that the ball would finally spill over the top. Only the materials provided were allowed to stop up the holes, plus any article of clothing being worn by a competitor. Once the Ping-Pong ball spilled over the top, the team was allowed to continue the race. Our team of four, with Scott Molina and Erin Baker, never did get the Ping-Pong ball to float over the top, but we were allowed to go after a certain time limit. The race director had included this challenge in order to spread the teams out at the start of the race.

THE RACECOURSE

The racecourse in a sprint-type or shorter adventure race may be marked, because teams cannot afford to be lost for any length of time, especially when the entire race is only expected to take a few hours to complete. The race is usually designed with a single TA to provide a central location for spectators. Special tests are usually located near the TA so that spectators can watch the fun.

For both short and long adventure races, the racecourse is often not divulged until just prior to the race, during the pre-race meeting the night before, or at a maximum one to two days before the race. The reason for this is in keeping with the spirit of adventure. Because the course is not divulged, no one can "practice" on it prior to the race. Racers are provided with maps and race directions that give instructions and/or map coordinates indicating locations, or checkpoints, the racers must travel to. In some MountainQuest races, as well as others, the maps and instructions are handed out when the clock starts, so that a team's abil-

Team Outlast receiving maps and race instructions at the Raid Gauloises 2000.
© 2000 Don Gabrielson

ity to quickly and accurately map the checkpoint locations and plot the course to take will play a part in when they leave the starting line.

At a MountainQuest race near Grand Junction, Colorado, teams plotted their checkpoints on their maps and began to leave the start area. One team, much to our consternation as race directors, took off in the exact opposite direction from everyone else, not even realizing that the other teams had gone in the other direction. Fortunately, several hours later they returned to the starting line after realizing their mistake, and were able to continue on.

In most races the course is not marked as it is in a triathlon, and teams must rely on their navigation skills to select the best course to follow. Other races may incorporate a combination of marked and unmarked sections, primarily for safety reasons or permit requirements. For example, jungle navigation can be very difficult, and it may not be reasonable to allow teams to get lost for two days in what is predicted to be a five-day race. It also might be difficult, if not impossible, for race management to locate a team that becomes lost in the jungle.

An adventure race is designed so that teams travel through the course by navigating from checkpoint to checkpoint along the route. TAs are checkpoints where teams transition from one sport to another and refuel and restock their supplies. Sprint and weekend races often utilize a single TA, with teams coming into the same area each time they finish one segment of the race and transition to a new sport. In the longer adventure races, TAs are spread along the racecourse.

Only maps provided by the race organization are allowed for navigation so that each team has the same information for the race. Occasionally, a global positioning system (GPS) is also allowed in races as a navigational tool (see Chapter 9, "Navigation"). For example, both the Raid Gauloises and the Beast of the East have allowed GPS units in some of their races.

PRE-RACE GEAR CHECK

Prior to the start of an adventure race the team may be required to demonstrate that they have certain skills required for the race, and to show that they have the required gear for the race (see Appendix A for sample mandatory gear lists). During the skills test, race organizers generally check for knowledge in ropes and paddling, and the competitors might be asked to demonstrate ascending and descending on ropes, and knowledge of safety and rescue practices on the water (for example, racers might be asked to hit a target with a throw bag). Some races require signed certificates prior to the race that attest to the competitor's skill and ability to complete certain disciplines. Other races, such as the Raid Gauloises and the Salomon X-Adventure Race, require a signed note from a physician stating that the competitor is "medically able" to compete in the race.

Pre-race gear check at the Raid Gauloises 2000.
© 2000 Don Gabrielson

Note: The pre-race check-in is not the time to spring a new prototype tent or other gear on the race directors. You should discuss it with them prior to arrival at the race.

Some adventure races (Eco-Challenge, ELF Authentic Adventure Race, Expedition Mata Atlantica, and others) have environmental and/or cultural projects that competitors take part in during the days before or after the race. The Eco-Challenge and the EMA have participated in tree plantings and river cleanups, whereas the ELF has encouraged teams to select their own cultural exchange, whether scientific, artistic, educational, or civic in nature.

THE RACE START

It is not uncommon for a "prologue" to take place prior to the start of some adventure races. Prologues are designed to introduce competitors to a new sport, select a starting position for the race, or for some other reason particular to the race. The Eco-Challenge 2000 included a prologue the day before the start of the race that had competitors testing out their perahu outrigger canoes while making their way to the starting line. A prologue consisting of a short run at altitude was scheduled for the day before the start of the Raid Gauloises 2000. The prologue was included so that teams would be able to test their acclimatization to the high altitude and pace themselves accordingly on race day. However, the prologue was canceled at the last minute due to the large number of competitors already suffering from altitude sickness prior to the start of the race. The ELF Authentic Adventure Race 2000 also included a prologue the day before the official start of the race, with teams sailing and paddling outrigger canoes in a race to establish which teams would get to be in the prime starting position on race morning.

Most adventure races begin with a mass start, with all teams beginning at once. Sometimes, the race begins with what is termed a "LeMans" start, named after the start of the LeMans car race. In a LeMans start, teams begin all together with a short run to their waiting bikes or boats. This technique is often used to provide an exciting start to the race, and create a slight spread to the teams early in the race.

Away on foot at the start of Eco-Challenge 1997 in Australia.
© 1997 Dan Campbell

Occasionally, in a stage-type race, teams will be started with a time delay between each team. The time interval is simply subtracted from each team's finishing time to adjust for this time-delay start. The time-delay start may be used because the discipline that the race is starting with is, for example, mountain biking and teams are converging on a single track trail that cannot handle a large pack of riders, or, most often, because the race organizers want to try to ensure that the team that crosses the finish line first is the overall winner.

CHECKPOINTS

Checkpoints (sometimes called Passport Control) are locations along the race-course that teams must locate and travel to in order to make their way through the race. Each checkpoint must be arrived at in sequence, and the first team to go to all of the checkpoints in order and, finally, the finish line, is the winning team.

Checkpoints are often staffed by race volunteers who clock each team in and out and relay that information to the race organizers. In this way, each team's progress through the race is tracked. No aid is provided at a checkpoint except in an emergency. In some races the checkpoints may not all be staffed; instead, some may be marked with an orienteering flag or other similar marker, which has a unique punch or stamp attached. During the night, checkpoints are often marked by a cyalume (glow) stick to assist racers in locating them.

In many races, if a team misses a checkpoint, they may elect to return to the missed checkpoint and then continue to each checkpoint along the course, to avoid a penalty.

Getting the passport stamped at a checkpoint.
© 2000 Phil Mislinski

Most adventure races issue a "passport book" to each team. This book is carried with the team at all times and is provided to staff at each checkpoint so that it can be signed, or alternatively, if the checkpoint is not staffed, the passport book is punched by the team with the unique punch provided at the checkpoint location. In the Eco-Challenge 2000 our team found the passport belonging to Team Hi-Tec of the United States in a Ziploc bag floating in a bay. Although we turned it in at the next checkpoint, Team Hi-Tec had already passed the checkpoint ahead of us and was

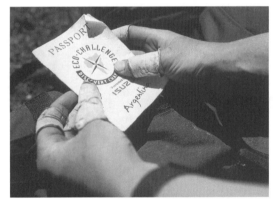

Passport to Adventure.
© 1999 Dan Campbell

forced to take a time penalty for losing the passport. If we had caught them before the checkpoint, we would have returned the passport to them—with a little good-humored bribery, of course.

TRANSITION AREAS

Transition areas are checkpoints where the teams' gear and food are available. Generally it signals the end of one discipline and the beginning of another. If the race is a supported race, the team's support crew will be waiting at the TA with food and the gear for the next discipline, as well as information about the next disciplines. The support crew will give the team any new maps and instructions or information about changes on the course (see Chapter 4, "The Support Crew").

In an unsupported race, the team gear is available but no support crew is waiting with hot food. The team has access to their gear and the opportunity to change into dry clothes and restock their food and water supply. Race management may also provide new maps and race instructions for the upcoming section of the race at the TA.

The clock continues to run while the team is in the TA, so the idea is to get what you need and continue on as quickly as possible. This becomes particularly important in the shorter races, which have a rapid pace and the race can be won or lost by minutes, if not seconds. In longer adventure races expected to take many days, teams might choose to rest or sleep in the TA for a while before continuing on. Each team will make the decision on how long to spend in the TA based on their race goals, time of day, and the overall condition of each team

A moment of rest in the transition area.
© 2000 Dan Campbell

member. For example, in a long race, if the TA is reached during the night and the team is in need of rest, it might be a good place to sleep for a few hours. There is likely to be shelter at the TA, and if the race is supported, the support crew is available to take care of details, such as refilling hydration packs, while the team sleeps.

It is important to be organized in the TA. A plastic gear box, 30 gallons or larger, is a good way to organize your gear. With a little creativity, the gear box can be compartmentalized to separate different gear—use plastic sheets or cardboard to create partitions in the box. Many racers place different sports items in color-coded and/or labeled bags to keep them separate and make them easy to grab during the transition. Clear bags are good to use because the items stored inside can be seen. For further organization, attach a clear plastic sheet to the inside lid of the gear box and secure it with duct tape on three sides, leaving the edge at the top (when the box is open) untaped. This creates a great place to store small items or food so that you can quickly see them.

DARK ZONES

"Dark zones" are implemented in many races for safety purposes. Most often a dark zone is associated with a section of whitewater. During a dark zone, teams are not allowed to continue until the time specified by race management. Teams are made aware of dark zones prior to the race so that team strategies can be decided. However, occasionally it is necessary for the race organizers to implement a new dark zone. For example, in the Raid Gauloises 2000, there was a political uprising in Nepal during the race, resulting in concern for competitors' safety when traveling at night during certain sections of the race. The Eco-Challenge attempts to design its races so that there are no dark zones. In the Eco-Challenge 2000, teams were required to be off the river in a whitewater section by sundown but were not prohibited from portaging along the river during the night if they chose to. Travel along the river was nearly impossible, and the local wooden sampan canoes were so heavy that no one took up the challenge.

ALTERNATE COURSE
AND RACE
CUTOFF TIMES

A unique feature of adventure racing is the provision of an alternate racecourse for those teams that are unlikely to complete the entire race in the allotted time. Time cutoffs will have been established for certain sections along the course in an attempt to keep the teams from spreading out too far across the racecourse and to ensure that all teams finish the race by a certain time. Teams not making these cutoff times may find themselves either being transported by race management and skipping a section of the course or continuing on an altered or shortened course. In this way, teams are allowed to continue and finish the race, generally with a new altered course ranking. Because the overall finishing percentage for adventure races is historically low (often less than 50 percent), these altered courses become important.

Occasionally, through no fault of the teams, the race situation changes significantly due to weather, and race management will decide to alter the racecourse. This decision may not affect all teams; often a few teams make it through a section before the dangerous conditions arrive, so only some of the teams will proceed on the altered course.

PENALTIES

Penalties may be assessed to a team during an adventure race. These can range from penalties for loss of a passport book or mandatory gear item, or penalties for poor sportsmanship. For example, at the Mild Seven Outdoor Quest 2000, one team was penalized for mistreating a race volunteer. At the inaugural FogDog 24-Hour Adventure Race 2000, one team was given a two-hour penalty for going off the designated course in one section. Penalties are given in the form of a suitable addition of time to the finishing time, or may be given by having the team "serve" the penalty at the nearest checkpoint to the infraction.

Adventure racing is still a fairly young sport, at least in the United

States, and many race structures exist. There is no single standardized race format, or standardized disciplines making up an adventure race, and all of the new and creative race formats springing up each year are a welcome addition to the sport.

TEAM COMPOSITION

Teams typically consist of from three to five members, of which at least one is of the opposite sex. Although teams, and particularly coed teams, have been the standard in the early years of adventure racing, many races now allow single-sex teams and solo competitors. The Sea to Summit Race, a three-day stage race started at Whistler Mountain, British Columbia, Canada, successfully combines team and solo competitors. Many competitors feel that the team aspect is an integral and important part of adventure racing, but there are many who, for various reasons, prefer to challenge themselves and nature by going it solo. Solo competitors are often not allowed in the continuous longer adventure races because some race directors are concerned about the safety issues. Other race directors simply feel that doing an adventure race solo is counter to the original spirit of the sport and ignores the important role of the team to the overall adventure race experience.

The majority of coed teams are all male with a single female. However, in the Eco-Challenge 1999, Team Atlas Snowshoes Rubicon—going against the norm—was composed of three females (Robyn Benincasa, Rebecca Rusch, and Cathy Sassin) and one male (Ian Adamson), and finished in a respectable fourth place.

The requirements of the Raid Gauloises, which state that the team must have at least one female, also allow for all-female teams to compete. Each year, one or two all-female teams compete in the Raid Gauloises, but most of the teams are composed of four men and one woman.

The Salomon X-Adventure Race series, held in Europe for several years, made its debut in the United States in 2000. The race format involves coed teams of four, but only three team members compete at a time, with the fourth providing support. The fourth team member can then be substituted in at the next TA. This unique format ensures a fast-paced race, with occasional rest for each team member.

Most adventure races require that teams wear a race jersey or have race patches on their clothing throughout the entire race. The jerseys and patches identify the race, the race sponsors, and the team number. In many races (Salomon X-Adventure, Hi-Tec) teams are required to wear race jerseys provided by the race organization. The jersey must be worn on the outside of clothing and paddling life jackets at all times. Some races even require that the jersey be worn over the backpack so that the team number is visible from the back.

The authors, with teammates Erin Baker and Scott Molina, show off their race jerseys before the start of the Mild Seven Outdoor Quest 2000.

The Raid Gauloises and the Eco-Challenge, as well as other adventure races, provide each competitor with race patches that must be sewn onto each piece of outerwear clothing that might be worn in the race. Many teams elect to sew a single set of the patches onto a lightweight jersey that can be worn over clothing throughout the race, such as shirts, jackets, and lifejackets. Teams get creative in making the most lightweight jersey possible, using materials such as mosquito netting and mesh football jerseys. Using a single jersey throughout the race is often easier than sewing the large number of required patches onto each piece of race clothing. Also, removal of the patches from clothing after the race can often ruin the clothes so that they cannot be used again in another race.

RACE LOCATION

The premier expedition-length adventure races, such as the Eco-Challenge and the Raid Gauloises, historically take place in exotic locations around the world. Locations have included New Caledonia, Lesotho, and Ecuador (Raid Gauloises); and Morocco, Australia, and British Columbia (Eco-Challenge).

Other annual races, such as the Southern Traverse in New Zealand, Expedition Mata Atlantica in Brazil, and the Raid Aventura in Argentina, take place in the same country each year, but the location within the country changes. Many adventure races, from short to long, have frequently been held in the same location each year, particularly in the United States and Canada. Examples include the Beast of the East in Virginia, the Nantahala Outdoor Center Adventure Race in North Carolina, the Pathfinder Challenge in Illinois, and some of the races in the Raid the North Adventure Race series in Canada.

In the United States, adventure races usually take place on lands under the auspices of the U.S. Forest Service, Bureau of Land Management, and in state and county parks. Any location with enough navigable water and trails provides a potential adventure racing location. The inaugural Wild Onion 2000 race took place in downtown Chicago, introducing the idea of an urban adventure race—still with the idea of adventure and exploration.

The world of adventure.
© 2000 Dan Campbell

CHAPTER 3

TEAM ASPECTS OF ADVENTURE RACING

© 1996 Dan Campbell

The team plays a vital role in adventure racing. Although many shorter races allow solo competitors, most of the long adventure races still only allow teams to compete for safety as well as traditional reasons. In adventure racing the only finish that counts is one where your entire team finishes the race intact. If someone is forced to drop out for any reason, the team becomes unranked. Under certain circumstances the remaining members of the team will be allowed to continue; in other situations, the race is over for the entire team. Your teammates are the people who will help to ensure your successful journey to the finish line. Therefore, the selection of your teammates will be among the most important decisions you make in adventure racing.

SELECTING TEAMMATES

How do you select good teammates? Consider four key criteria: compatible goals, compatible personalities, individual strengths, and comparable fitness levels. Begin by determining what your personal goals are for the race. Do you want to put together a team that can win, a team that can finish in the top ten, or a team that can simply finish? Do you want to approach the race as a very serious undertaking, or something that can provide a wonderful experience that you and your teammates can have fun doing?

Sticking together.
© 1997 Dan Campbell

You need to understand and be clear about what you want from the race before you can find people to join you. Why? Because it is crucial to find teammates who have the same goals as you. If you just want to have fun and finish, and you team up with others who have a "win at all costs" attitude, the team is not likely to succeed or meet anyone's goals. In addition, the team is apt to feel unnecessary stresses during the race.

Probably even more important than compatibility of goals is compatibility of personalities. Do you like this person? You will be spending a lot of time together, under very stressful conditions—when you are tired and probably less tolerant than usual. It is important to find teammates who you really enjoy being with. If you want to have a positive experience during the race, look for people who have had good race experiences in the past. Shy away from those who tend to consistently blame other teammates for bad race experiences. These are people who consistently are "victims" and don't take responsibility for making the race experience pleasant. In fact, if you do choose to race with them, it is likely that you will be the next person blamed and talked about.

Ask yourself these questions about a prospective teammate:

1.   Is the person too talkative/not talkative enough?

2. Does he or she seem too intense, or not intense enough?

3. Do they laugh at the same kinds of things you do?

4. How do they respond to challenges/difficulty?

5. Are they good team players?

Everyone's personality will be amplified during a race, so be honest about this person now. It could save you from having an unpleasant race experience. Early on in our racing career, for example, we contemplated racing with an individual with very strong athletic skills but decided against it because we were uncomfortable with the types of jokes this person told.

Another criterion for selecting teammates is to evaluate your strengths and weaknesses and look for people who can add needed strength to the team. For example, for the Raid Gauloises 2000 in Tibet and Nepal, we knew that the race was going to involve a lot of whitewater paddling. The race organization for the Raid Gauloises is largely French, and we had learned from previous races that having someone on the team who could speak French was a big advantage. As a result, we were looking for a paddling expert who could speak French. As luck would have it, Billy Mattison, former captain of Team Vail (winners of the Eco-Challenge 1998), was available, because his team did not get a spot in the Raid Gauloises that year. Billy is one of the sport's best whitewater guides and speaks fluent French!

The final criterion and probably the least important overall in a long race, is to find people with similar fitness levels and capabilities. This criterion becomes much more important for the shorter, sprint-type races. It certainly helps to have people who are similar in fitness and speed in all sports. However, in a long race, you can be sure that at one time or another different teammates will experience low points that will keep them from performing at their absolute best. This is when the ability of the team to respond and creatively determine ways to help the teammate feel better and go faster is the defining factor on the success or failure of the race. This ability will be determined more by the overall personality and goals of the team than by the fitness level of each team member.

JOINING AN EXISTING TEAM

When you begin racing you might have the opportunity to join an existing team. Here is a list of important questions to ask if someone invites you to join their team:

1. Is the team financed? If not, how much would I be expected to pay?

2. Who else is on the team?

3. What is the experience of the other team members?

4. Has this team raced together before? If so, what has your experience been?

5. What are the team's strengths and weaknesses?

6. What are your goals for the race? Do you expect to win or just hope to finish?

7. How are team decisions made?

8. What would you expect my contribution to the team to be?

Find prospective teammates through interactive "find a teammate" databases provided by many adventure racing Web sites, or by contacting the race director of a race you are interested in doing. Race directors will do what they can to match people up with teams in need of a teammate. Other sources for teammates include adventure race camps, multisport clubs, and references from other racers.

If possible, meet with the team to see how it works out before the race. It is not necessary, or maybe even advisable, to go on a training session when you first meet them. Training the first time you meet can create unnecessary anxiety, and, if your personalities don't mesh, the training experience can be frustrating enough to prevent you from wanting to get into adventure racing at all. The first meeting should be informal, short, and relaxed. Meet the team or prospective teammate for a beer or lunch and see how your first meeting goes—you will be able to tell very quickly whether you would enjoy racing with them.

TRAINING TOGETHER

If you find that you like the people on the team, then try getting together for a training hike. Training hikes are generally nonthreatening, and everyone has the chance to talk and get to know each other. It is a great opportunity to see how the team works together and whether general fitness levels are matched. Talk with the team about everyone's abilities in the other sports. If, for example, you join a team of expert paddlers who can't mountain bike well, and you are an expert mountain biker who does not paddle, that doesn't mean that together you won't make a good team. Each team member just needs to be aware of each other's abilities and weaknesses so there are no false expectations resulting in disappointment.

Some teams, but not all, train together. Many teams are formed over the

Internet (such as the legendary Team Eco-Internet), or through mutual friends and racers, and, because teammates live in different areas, they do not have the luxury of training together. We have frequently raced with teammates we have never trained with. This has never been a problem, because we have communicated with them frequently via e-mail and phone, and because we usually know (through other racers) what their skill level and personality is.

TEAM ROLES

The team captain is usually the person who has secured the team spot in the race. Many times the team captain is also the person who has obtained sponsorship funding for the team. The team captain generally has the overall responsibility for putting the team together with help from existing teammates; ensuring that all paperwork for the race is completed; ensuring all teammates have the requisite paperwork (passport, visa, medical, media forms); and seeing to it that all race fees are paid (either through sponsors or a shared responsibility among teammates).

TEAMMATE HONESTY

At the Mild Seven Outdoor Quest 2000, we teamed with triathlon legends Scott Molina and Erin Baker. Their athletic ability is far beyond ours, but they were interested in trying an adventure race and willing to give it a go with us. We were very clear with them about our lack of speed in a fast-paced stage race, and they were equally candid with us about their lack of experience in paddling and inline skating. As a result, we had a wonderful experience and enjoyed racing together.

If the team captain is the contact person for the team sponsor, the captain will be responsible for administering the sponsor money and any prize money the team might win. Most people entering the sport of adventure racing have not had the need to deal with sponsorship in their racing career. However, because of the cost of competing, particularly in the long adventure races, sponsorship becomes important. Consequently, most teams will find themselves seeking out sponsorships or partnerships to help with race entry fees and travel expenses and obtaining the gear necessary to race.

Gear and clothing are much easier to obtain than financial support. Most companies are looking for a return on their investment through marketing opportunities, relevant utilization of equipment and clothing during the race, and product feedback. Because it is so difficult to guarantee television or media coverage of the team during the race, it is more important to focus on providing marketing opportunities and being a positive representative of the sponsor. This can include presentations and motivational talks after the race. If you do obtain a race sponsor, think of creative ways to deliver even more than they expect— and don't forget to get pictures during the race.

The team captain (or an appointed team member) will compile an up-to-date listing of the required gear for the race and identify who is responsible for each piece of gear. The team captain has the ultimate responsibility for making sure that all team members have read the race rules and that the team abides by them.

The team captain will often put together a notebook containing all of the important race information including (1) race management contact numbers, (2) airline arrival information for each team member, if applicable, (3) team member emergency contact information, (4) copies of the race newsletters and rules, and (5) a copy of the final mandatory gear list with who is responsible for what team gear.

During the race, the team captain may or may not assume the role of leader. For many teams, the navigator takes on the role of leader in the field. However, if the team has an issue that needs to be resolved, the team captain will solicit input from team members but will assume ultimate responsibility for resolving things quickly.

The team member who will take responsibility for navigation should be identified before the start of the race. If the team is lucky enough to have two or more experienced navigators, they will probably be happy to trade off the responsibility during the race. The most experienced person will start as the lead navigator, while other team members with navigation experience will provide backup and assistance and be ready to step in when the lead navigator needs to take a rest. Only one person should assume the lead navigation position at a time, or arguments might ensue.

Other team roles that might be identified before the race include selection of a safety person and a medical person. When issues of safety arise, the team will discuss them together. However, selecting one person to make the final decision on whether the team should proceed with a course of action can be helpful. The safety person might also be the most skilled person in the use of ropes and will have the responsibility to observe each team member and ensure that the equipment is secured and safe before any rope work is undertaken.

The medical person will be the most medically trained individual on the team and might be given the authority to evaluate the condition of an ailing team member and make the recommendation on whether they should continue. They might be given the authority to make the decision when to open the emergency radio to summon help for an injured teammate. The reason for doing this is the recognition of everyone's desire to stay in the race, and sometimes when they would place their own health in jeopardy. All of these roles should be discussed before the race.

Two of the most frequently asked questions of female adventure racers are: "What is it like to be the only female on a team with males?" and "What is your role on the team?" One of the truly unique aspects of adventure racing is that men and women are racing as equal members of a team. For many competitors, male and female, this is the first time ever really racing together, side-by-side. Many adventure racers come from a competitive background that includes separate racing categories or teams for men and women. In the long, expedition-length races, the athletic differences between men and women are not obvious, with both men and women having moments when they are strong and moments when they need assistance from teammates. In the shorter races, where speed is a premium, the woman on a team may feel added pressure to try to perform up to a level equal to the men. Yet, in adventure racing, with the understanding that the entire team needs to finish together, each team member helps the other, regardless of being male or female. The only aspect of being a female adventure racer that sometimes causes frustration is that most adventure clothing and equipment is currently made for men!

BEFORE
THE RACE

Teamwork really begins prior to the start of the race. There is a saying in adventure racing that sometimes the hardest part is getting to the starting line. The

HOW MUCH WEIGHT SHOULD YOU CARRY?

A 130-pound female would ideally carry no more than 10 to 15 percent of her body weight, or 13 to 19 pounds. Men typically have a much higher weight-to-muscle-mass ratio and can carry more. A 170-pound male can carry 15 to 25 percent of his body weight, or roughly 25 to 40 pounds.

team needs to be able to work together to make sure that all team and personal mandatory gear is assembled, bikes are in working order, and everyone is prepared and understands the race rules and instructions.

Before the race, identify who is carrying what pieces of team mandatory gear, and select what additional items you need to carry. For instance, not everyone needs to carry a bike pump and a bike tool kit (unless required by the race). Select the person who has the best and lightest of these items and only carry those. Try not to duplicate gear that the team only needs one or two of. Division of weight within the team is very important. Many teams elect to distribute as much of the weight among its male team members as possible. This is not because the female team members are weaker but because they weigh less and the percentage of weight they can carry without diminishing their performance is smaller.

If the race instructions have been given out prior to the race, take the time to go through them carefully together. Identify what you will need to get rid of and pick up at each transition area, and consider making a list that you can tape to the inside of the team captain's gear box so that when you arrive at the TA, the team captain can read the list out loud to remind everyone quickly what they need to do. For example, when you finish a biking section and begin a trekking section, the note might read: "Take food for three days. Take helmet and climbing gear for ropes section. Take trekking poles and mountain jacket [other mandatory gear for trekking section]. Remember passport."

In the longer races, cutoff times may have been set at various points during the race to ensure that everyone completes the race in a certain time frame. The team should look carefully at the cutoff times and determine whether there is a possibility for the team to make the checkpoint before the cutoff. If the team thinks it is possible, they might decide to go really hard up to that point to be sure they make it. If the team feels that there is no way to make the cutoff without overtaxing team members and potentially jeopardizing the rest of the race, they might choose to go at a slower pace and conserve the team's energy. Another scenario in some of the twenty-to-thirty-hour races is the potential for teams to get backed up and be forced to wait at the ropes section. The team might decide to go really hard to get to the ropes section before the other teams arrive to make sure they do not have to wait. These are some of the important decisions that need to be discussed thoroughly as a team.

DURING
THE RACE

The successful adventure racing team develops a race strategy and then works together during the race to make it happen. For the sprint and stage adventure races, the strategy might simply be to go as hard as possible from the start of the race to the finish. Many teams will elect to use towing systems for running and biking right from the beginning of the race. In the longer adventure races, the starting pace will be more moderate and towing systems will be used more when the need arises (although many top teams elect to begin towing very early).

Occasionally the team will need to work together to assist another teammate. There are many things that team members can do to help one another out, such as assigning a task to do, towing or pushing, taking a teammate's backpack, and redistributing weight among backpacks.

If someone is slowing down on the trekking section, it may be helpful to assign them a task, such as putting them in the front to set the pace. A teammate who is having difficulty keeping up will often pick up the pace when put in the front to lead the way. Leading may take their mind off whatever is making them slow down. When a struggling teammate is placed at the back of the team, either on the bike or on foot, they often begin to feel worse mentally and fall off of the back even more.

In adventure racing other team members can, and often do, tow or push the other person. This is an effective means of maintaining the team's over-all rate of progress on both the bike and the trekking sections. Even the top adventure racing teams do this—sometimes right from the start of the race. A trekking tow system can be as simple as a section of thin surgical tubing tied to the lead person's backpack and clipped with a carabiner to the waistband of the trailing team member. Using a carabiner to clip to the trailing team member allows that person to quickly remove the tow system if the terrain becomes uneven or difficult to follow someone through.

It is also possible, while hiking, for the struggling team member to simply hold onto a strap on the stronger person's backpack and be pulled along and/or to be pushed from behind by another team member.

Towing while on the bike is also an important team aspect of adventure racing. A simple bike tow system is described in detail in Chapter 5, "Mountain Biking." Another technique, if the team is riding on either an open road or wide trail is for one team member to ride next to the struggling team member and push them by placing their hand on the back of the other's backpack. The amount of assistance this technique can provide is surprising. Alternatively, the struggling team member can ride just to the side and slightly behind a stronger rider and hang on to their backpack, shirttail, or whatever is available. All of these towing techniques require practice before the race in order for them to be efficient and effective.

The team must work together to find solutions to help someone who is struggling. A teammate who is feeling strong might take the struggling person's backpack for a while, or take items from that person's backpack and redistribute them among all of the other team members. Getting the weight off of a teammate's back, even for a short period of time, can do a lot to assist in the person's recovery and mental state.

The team will be even more successful if they can prevent any teammate from feeling poorly enough to have their performance affected. Set a pace that is comfortable for everyone. Notice when teammates begin to get quiet if they are normally talkative or when they begin to fall behind, and offer assistance quickly. The mental aspects of racing are often the most important, so remain positive and supportive. At some point in the race, you might need help yourself.

What are some things that the team can do to make sure everyone feels strong? Each time one person takes a drink, they should yell, "Drinking!" as a reminder for everyone to drink. Then notice if everyone does—a teammate who is not drinking enough will eventually become dehydrated and suffer performance problems that could turn into serious health problems. Notice who is not refilling their bottle or hydration bladder (a vinyl water reservoir with a tube reaching from the reservoir to the person's mouth) when everyone else is, and try to help them remember to drink more often. Offer them your bottle when you are drinking. Consider having one person on the team set a countdown timer on their watch for every fifteen minutes to remind everyone to drink. That works well for us when we race.

It is always a good idea to share your food when you take something out to eat, especially when you notice a team member beginning to have difficulty; they might need food. Break off a piece of food to give them, or pass them the food so they can take some. When a team member begins to feel bad, the effort involved in taking food out for themselves sometimes prevents him or her from eating, and their health and athletic performance begin to spiral downhill quickly.

The team needs to be moving together as a unit at all times. Stay together always, within sight and shouting distance. In one race, our team got split up during a bike section and the two team members way out front did not notice that one of the trailing team members got a flat tire. Unfortunately, the only repair kit and pump were on the bike of one of the team members out front. We lost a lot of time and energy trying to catch and bring the leading team members back to help. In another race in France, we observed one team member continue on his bike while two others stopped to fix a flat tire. The first rider did not know that he needed to make a turn at the bottom of the hill and continued on. When the other team members finished fixing the flat, they continued on down the hill and made the turn, not realizing that their teammate had missed the turn. The team never recovered and ended up dropping out of the race as a result.

When the team is looking for a trail or specific marker that you know is nearby, identify a strategy to use. For example, a few team members can sleep while the others look around the area. If all team members are going to look, decide how you are going to do it and stick to the plan. An example would be to have everyone walk out in a different direction for ten minutes from the starting point—returning to the same point at the end of that time. During the Southern Traverse in 1997, the team did not use this strategy. We could not find the trail at one point, so everyone on the team went a different direction, convinced that they knew the correct way. The area was particularly rough terrain, with thick brush everywhere, making it difficult to move or see very far. Before we realized what had happened, the entire team had scattered and it took nearly two hours to find each other and regroup.

As with everything in an adventure race, the idea is for the team to constantly be moving forward. Practice removing your jacket and putting it on again while moving so that you don't have to stop the team each time you need to do something. Ask a teammate to put your discarded item (hat, gloves, jacket) into your pack while you both continue to move. Run ahead a little if you need to relieve yourself. The team can slow their pace slightly while you catch up, maintaining the forward movement of the team. Remember, if the team stops for five minutes every hour in a twenty-four hour race, that adds up to two hours of time spent standing still!

The team offers many opportunities for fun and assistance. Think of ways to help each other out. After jumping across a stream, turn around and help your teammate across—it will pay off in dividends, both in return favors and in helping to maintain a positive attitude during the race. A team full of "individuals" will have a harder time succeeding in this team sport.

While racing in Patagonia in 2000, one of our teammates became concerned about her feet blistering and put on clean dry socks and shoes at the TA for the upcoming trek. A few miles out from the TA, the team was faced with a stream crossing. Without even hesitating, another team member told her to hop on his back for a piggyback ride across the stream. That's the kind of teammate you want to race with!

CHAPTER 4

THE SUPPORT CREW

© 2000 Dan Campbell

Not all races require the assistance of a team support crew, and, in fact, support crews are prohibited in some races, such as the Eco-Challenge. Many races do, however, require that one or two persons, and a vehicle capable of transporting all of the team gear between assistance points, support each team. For these races, the support crew becomes a vital part of a successful race.

HOW IMPORTANT IS YOUR SUPPORT CREW?

To reach the final transition area of the Raid Gauloises 2000, support crews had to drive for almost thirty hours. Teams were expected to take three days to reach the transition area, so many support crews detoured through Katmandu for a shower and a comfortable bed. However, the top teams took much less time to complete this leg of the race than expected. The combination of the detour time spent in Katmandu and flat tires on the support vehicles resulted in the first-place team, Salomon Land Rover, arriving at the transition area four hours ahead of their support team. Considering they arrived at the finish only an hour behind the leaders, this problem may have cost them the race.

A good support crew can help the race go smoothly, provide much-needed food, first aid, gear maintenance, and moral support, and limit the amount of time the team spends in the TA. It is important to select your support staff as carefully as you pick your teammates.

SELECTING YOUR SUPPORT CREW

Your support crew will often be family, friends, or other athletes wanting to learn about the sport of adventure racing. Occasionally it may be necessary to engage people you have never met, especially if you are racing far from home or in a country outside of the United States. The race director can be a good resource to help you find a support crew local to the race area. You can also contact local race sponsors—mountaineering, biking, or running stores and area sports clubs and gyms—that might be able to help you find a crew.

Here's what to look for in support team members:

▲ Ability to work well with others.
▲ Good organizational skills.
▲ Ability to endure some hardship (lack of sleep, inclement weather).
▲ Ability to lift and move boxes of gear and equipment.
▲ Ability to improvise and be flexible.
▲ Basic cooking ability.
▲ Bike maintenance skills.
▲ Good map-reading skills and sense of direction (so the crew will be waiting for you at the next transition area!).

If you have two support people for the race, it is extremely important that they get along and complement each other's skills. They will be dealing with less-than-perfect conditions for a large part of the race, so it is essential that they are able to work together well. The most successful support crews are those where tasks have been clearly divided; that way, each person knows what to do and what is expected of them. Usually, the division of tasks takes place naturally, but it is a good idea to have the support crew discuss it before the race so that they have definite and clear responsibilities.

During the Raid Gauloises 2000, all of the top support crews divided their jobs. Our team, Outlast, divided their tasks into cooking, camp organization, and first aid for one support member, and bike maintenance, bartering, and information gathering for the other. Interestingly enough, two of the other support crews of top finishing teams divided their tasks in the same way. Bartering and information gathering are important tasks because they are the only ways you may be able to resupply in certain areas, or learn of changes in team status on the course. Team Outlast's support crew had heard rumors that the course had been shortened before the last TA and, as a result, decided to skip the luxury of Katmandu and pushed on to arrive at the TA before the team.

During the race, your support crew will be interacting with other teams and support crews, race management, media, and spectators. A support crew that is well liked and respected reflects well on the team and on the team sponsor.

Support crewmembers need to be organizational heroes. Not only do they need to keep track of all of their own gear during the race, they need to be able to quickly locate whatever it is that the competitors request of them. All of this happens in a mad frenzied rush during the transition time, so it is important that the crew be able to respond quickly to multiple requests and pull the rabbit out of the hat!

The support crew is often working under less-than-ideal conditions—in rain, snow, or extreme heat, and with a lack of running water, showers, or toilet facilities. For long races it is important to select a crew that is comfortable with primitive camping. The support crew will likely be

A HELPING HAND

During the Raid Gauloises 2000, since the vehicles were prone to breaking down and maintenance was impossible for major problems, many teams swapped vehicles or drivers when needed. A good driver who could navigate, stay awake, and fix flat tires was worth their weight in gold. Team Saloman Land Rover accompanied Team Nokia, who had engine trouble, to the last transition. Team Nokia gave their vehicle and driver to Team Salomon Land Rover when Salomon's truck suffered a broken axle just after leaving the last transition. Team Outlast then gave their vehicle and driver to Nokia (now stranded), and finally after arriving at the finish Nokia arranged for a new vehicle and driver for Outlast.

tired and hungry, just like the competitors, throughout the race. For example, during the Raid Gauloises 2000, competitors traveled over 500 miles while support crews ended up traveling almost 2,000 miles by vehicle over very rough roads.

Support and transition at Salomon Winter Adventure Race 2000.
© 2000 Darrin Eisman

The crew will be packing and unpacking the team's transport vehicle many times during the race. This will require putting bicycles either into or on top of the vehicle, as well as potentially loading and unloading kayaks or canoes. The crew must be able to handle lifting and securing these items to the car quickly and efficiently. In addition, each competitor has a bag or box (or both) filled with clothing and gear for the race. All of these things must be taken out of, and then returned to, the vehicle at each TA.

A successful support crew is composed of people who can improvise when necessary. At the Raid Gauloises, our support crew's vehicle broke down between TAs while the team was doing a whitewater swim. The swim was taking teams an average of three to four hours to complete, so there was little time for the crew to pack the gear from the last TA and get to the new one. The crew was able to catch a ride part way from another support crew who did not expect to see their team for another day. From that point one crew member hauled gear over the ridge while the other ferried the rest by boat to the TA. Not only did they both make it before the team did, they also had much-needed hot food waiting for us.

It isn't necessary for the support crew to be able to cook gourmet meals for the team; however, a basic ability to cook in the outdoors is essential. This can simply mean as little as having hot water available for dehydrated foods or being ready with spaghetti when the team arrives. Again, the ability to improvise is key. For example, at one transition, our Raid Gauloises support crew met us

Rehydrating in the transition area.
© 1999 Darrin Eisman

SUPPORT CREW CAMARADERIE

Cooking and sharing meals or a snack with other support crews often takes place. At the Expedition Mata Atlantica (EMA) 1999 Brazil, while support crews were stuck for three days at a remote transition area with no news of the race, people began to party to relieve the stress. Most of the teams were from the local area and had elaborate kitchens and food. Too bad the team still got regular race fare— noodles, Gatorade, and PowerBars!

with spaghetti that they had cooked without a stove (because there was not enough fuel left to run the stove). They were able to "cook" the noodles by just placing the pot of water in the blazing sun (115°F). Equally important is that the support crew will be fixing meals for themselves during the race, so they need to be able to cook things they will enjoy eating.

Additional skills that are helpful are basic bike repair (fixing flats, changing tires, adjusting brakes), medical knowledge (treating blisters, wrapping sprains, cleaning and bandaging cuts),

The support crew caravan.
© 1995 Dan Campbell

and navigational ability. In many adventure races your support crew will receive the map and race instructions for the next race segment before you arrive at the TA. If your crew is knowledgeable in navigation, they can look at the maps, plot Universal Transverse Mercator (UTM) coordinates (see Chapter 9, "Navigation"), and give you a preliminary sketch of the best route to follow.

DURING THE RACE

What can the support team expect to be doing during the race? It is the team's responsibility to prepare the support crew for the race so they know:

What is expected of them.

What they will be doing.

Everyone's preferences on gear setups.

Who has medical problems.

Any dietary restrictions.

Whose gear belongs to whom.

Ideally, your crew is made up of people who understand adventure racing, and perhaps even race themselves. Let them know that they will be an important part of the team. They will be expected to work hard and be resourceful.

After the start of the race the crew is responsible for getting team gear to the next (and each successive) TA. The support crew experience is often referred to as the "race within the race"— the support crew sometimes struggles to stay ahead of the team.

At the beginning of the race, support teams will usually travel together in a caravan, until the race begins to spread out. Support crews are provided with their own maps and instructions to get to the next TA. Once at the TA they will be busy setting up tents, tarps, kitchen, bikes, and other gear so that the team will have a place to rest or sleep if necessary, change clothes, get warm, and prepare for the next event. The crew will need to have each competitor's gear box and other bags set out for easy access. Once everything is ready for the team, the support crew needs to make sure that sponsor banners are displayed in the TA if appropriate.

If the weather is bad the gear will need to be in tents or under other cover, with enough space so that each competitor has plenty of room to maneuver. In 1997 it rained and snowed continuously throughout a seven-day race in Montana. Our support crew became famous for the tent city and "sauna" they constructed at each TA. They set up three tents facing inward toward the team van. Then the "common area" was covered with a large tarp secured to the tops of the van and over the tents, providing a central area for cooking. Tarps were laid down as a "floor" over the entire area to prevent us from slogging around in the mud. One tent was set up with a propane heater, five chairs (one for each competitor), and a table. The team was ushered to this tent when they arrived to eat and get warm, get briefed on the upcoming event, and go over the new maps and race instructions.

A large portion of the support crew's time will be spent waiting . . . and waiting . . . and waiting some more for the team to arrive. Unfortunately, at many races there is very little information available about the teams' whereabouts, condition, or expected arrival time. Fortunately, this is the time when the support crews get to know one another and create their own fun.

Tent city, the transition area at Raid Gauloises 2000.
© 2000 Don Gabrielson

SUPPORT CREW PRANKSTERS

At Expedition Mata Atlantica 1999, the first leg of the race took almost three times longer than predicted. Over the course of three days, only two teams arrived. Then at midnight of the third night, three lights appeared on the hill. The whole camp was up, cheering, blowing horns, mad with anticipation. Everyone waited with baited breath at the camp boundary. Finally, amid much fanfare, the three support crew members arrived. To ease the tension, the three had sneaked away from camp so they could arrive and provide a much-needed chuckle.

When the team finally arrives, the crew should

1. Give team members food, water, and beverages such as sport drinks and colas.
2. Brief the team on the upcoming segment.
3. Check each team member's general health and administer first aid.
4. Resupply packs with food and water.
5. Read mandatory gear list aloud.
6. Keep track of time spent in TA and communicate to team.

The crew should have hot and cold drinks and hot food available, if possible, when the team arrives. This is not easy to pull off because the support crew might not know when the team will arrive. The support crew might be told that their team just passed the final checkpoint before the TA and that they are on their way in to the TA. Even if other teams have been taking five hours to complete this last section, your team might get lost or decide to stop and sleep before continuing on to the TA. As a result, food that has been prepared too early might go to waste (or, hopefully, be shared with a team that surprises its support crew by coming in early!). It is important for the support crew to at least keep hot water available so that dehydrated foods can be prepared quickly. Many support crews use a large (1-gallon) hot Thermos to keep water hot for long periods of time in the field. Timing the preparation of the food with the arrival of the team becomes an art form of its own.

Prior to the race let your crew know of any special needs you have or things you want to have available at the TA. The team should discuss with the crew the food that they would like to have available and the way the TA should be set up. At the Southern Traverse in New Zealand our support crew had an array of food spread out on card tables so that we could quickly grab what we wanted as we came into the TA. The support crew should continue to bring food to the team during the transition time—this is the competitors' main opportunity to replenish their depleted bodies.

While the team is eating, the support crew needs to tell them what the next event will be and provide any other available information, such as the weather forecast, expected elevation gain in the next section, and the anticipated duration of the event, so that the team can think about and gather what they need. The crew should read the mandatory gear list for the upcoming segment of the race aloud so that everyone will know what he or she needs to have with them for the next section of the race. Toward the end of a long race, it is helpful for the support crew to pack the gear for tired or disoriented team members to assist them in getting out of the TA quicker.

The support crew should replenish each racer's hydration system (bladder or bottles) and place it in the backpack—ready for the next race segment. They should, based on their knowledge of the estimated length of the next event, place the competitor's prepackaged food bags (see Chapter 13, "Fuel for Racing") in each competitor's backpack, along with any special requests for the section.

Throughout the transition it is important for the support crew to remind the team of passing time. Set a watch timer for five or ten minutes and remind the team that they have been in the TA for ten minutes, twenty minutes, and so on. It is very easy for the team to get comfortable in the TA, and the support team has the very important job of getting the team in and out of there as quickly as possible.

Before the team leaves the TA, the crew should read the mandatory gear list once more out loud and check to make sure the team has the race passport (if required) before they leave the TA. During one race our team left the TA without the passport and, only by luck, realized it just about the time the support crew was spotted refueling the car at a gas station on their way to the next TA. We were able to get their attention, get the passport, and continue on. Without this bit of luck we would have been forced to wait at the next checkpoint for someone to get a new passport for us, transport our original one to us, or take a time penalty.

After the team leaves the TA, the race within the race begins all over again for the support crew. Competitor gear is sorted and put away (or if wet, thrown into a bag to clean and dry later, if time permits). Tents and tarps are taken down, dishes washed and packed. Bikes, boats, gear boxes, and bags are loaded into the team vehicle. Then the support crew is off to find the next TA and get set up before the team arrives.

Obviously, the support crew is an integral part of the team and it is important to have a happy crew! Be prepared to cover the cost of your crew's food and expenses during the race, and possibly pay them for their assistance. Work out the details before the race and have the crew keep a log of what they spend so they can be reimbursed after the race. In the end, their experience during the race will be rewarding and produce many memories to be shared with the team after the race.

SUGGESTED SUPPORT TEAM GEAR

Repair Items
Clothespins
Needle and thread
Safety pins
Scissors
Superglue
Duct tape
Strapping tape
Clear packing tape

Office Supplies
Highlighter pens
Pencils
Pencil sharpener
Pens
Eraser
Whiteout
Ruler with inches/centimeters
Small notebook/index cards

Biking/Trekking
Batteries (all sizes)
Spare tires/tubes
Handlebar tape
Spare trekking shoes for
    each racer
Extra sunglasses

Team Camping
Lantern(s)
Tarps
Parachute chord
Large tent(s)
Matches/spare lighter
Folding chairs
  (1 per racer)
Extra duffels to sort gear
Stove/fuel
Personal gear
Small tent
Sleeping pad
Boots/shoes/sandals
Leather work gloves
Small axe
Sun hat/sunglasses
Folding knife/
   Leatherman Tool
Flashlight/headlamp
Warm clothes/rain gear
Compass
GPS
Neck pillow (for car sleeping)
Sunscreen
Water purification system
Toilet paper/small shovel
Camera/film
Washcloth/towel

Kitchen
Wash basin (collapsible)
Dish soap
Scrubbie
Large cooler
Plastic cups/bowls/plates
Plastic cutlery
Can opener
Wooden spoons
Large knife
Large cook pot
Large skillet
Large Thermos (1 gallon)
Small Ziploc baggies
Large Ziploc baggies
Trash bags (heavy)
Assorted Tupperware
Potholder
Paper towels
Measuring cup
Collapsible water container

Health/Hygiene
Washcloths
Small towels
Soap
Aloe Vera
DEET/insect repellant
Cortisone cream
Sunscreen
Self-adhering Coban
   bandages
Athletic tape
Baby wipes
Antibacterial
   hand sanitizer
Full first-aid kit

PART TWO

THE
DISCIPLINES

CHAPTER 5

MOUNTAIN BIKING

Mountain biking is one of the core disciplines of adventure racing. The sprint adventure races and the expedition-length adventure races both include mountain biking because large distances can be covered on a mountain bike compared with other modes of travel.

Historically, bike sections of adventure races consist of dirt and fire or 4 × 4 roads, nontechnical single track with lots of long, uphill climbs. You could encounter sand, mud, and stream crossings on the bike route. Some races will include single-track riding, but for the most part the riding is not overly technical, except for short sections. Many bike sections require that competitors "hike-a-bike," in other words, push their bikes through sections clogged with logs, rocks, or up very steep inclines or through sections when conditions are just too muddy for riding.

The technical section at Salomon X-Adventure North America 2000.
© 2000 Salomon N.A./Thomas Zuccareno

The percentage of time you will be biking can vary, but a general rule of thumb is that at least one-third of the entire time in races of two to twenty-four hours will be spent mountain biking. In a typical Hi-Tec race, the mountain bike section will be 7 to 15 miles, whereas in an expedition-length race you could encounter multiple bike rides of up to 90 miles, taking more than twenty-four hours to complete. Mountain biking can account for big blocks of racing time—and, although it may be difficult if not impossible to paddle at night, it is completely possible to bike at night, so expect long rides that will often take you through the night.

EQUIPMENT

In addition to the mountain bike, other equipment that may be required can include a bike helmet, front and rear lights, tool kit, and spare bike tubes.

BIKES

Mountain bikes used in adventure races typically have, at a minimum, front suspension. Many adventure racers ride dual-suspension mountain bikes. The merits of both are debatable, but at the least, a good front-suspension bike is recommended because eventually you will be riding over some rough terrain. The Raid Gauloises 2000 required the use of front-suspension bikes and because of the very long, rocky descents in the race, dual-suspension bikes were strongly recommended. Many racers opted to add a shock-absorbing seat post to simulate rear suspension. This provided a relatively inexpensive way to add additional shock absorption for the race.

The most common frames are composed of aluminum or steel. Modern aluminum bike frames are stronger and stiffer than steel frames of similar weight and are designed to last for hundreds of thousands of miles. Titanium frames cost more, but because they are lightweight, the extra expense might be worth it. Whatever bike type you choose, the most important thing is to get one that fits and is comfortable. Select a mountain bike with adequate clearance between the top tube and you. Straddle the bike and make sure you have a minimum of 4 inches of clearance.

Recently, the advent of cross bikes has begun to make its way into adventure racing. Cross bikes are hybrid bikes that are lighter weight than a mountain bike. They have wheels that are more akin to those of a road bike, but with flat handlebars like a mountain bike. The dimensions of the cross bike are very similar to a road bike, but cross bikes are designed for less technical off-road riding and some road riding. Team Salomon Eco-Internet of the United States rode to victory in the Eco-Challenge 2000 on cross bikes. Whether this trend continues remains to be seen; many races (the Mild Seven Outdoor Quest 2000, for one) do not allow cross bikes. Tandem bikes are typically prohibited from use in adventure races.

BIKE TIRES

An important consideration for racing is the type of tires you have on your mountain bike. These can range from "knobby" tires to "slicks" to solid tires. Any size of tire will fit on a mountain bike wheel. Thinner profile tires (1.5 to 2.0 inches) with a smaller "knob" are an excellent choice for most adventure races. Tires that tend to throw mud off quickly and easily are strongly recommended because it is very likely that you will be riding through mud at some point in your racing career. The Mild Seven Outdoor Quest 2000 required competitors to have tires with a minimum width of 1.8 inches.

The large knobby tires that most new mountain bikes come with are fine for most people getting into adventure racing. They provide a large base and grip so that the racer has a high degree of confidence when riding off-road. Many racers use semi-slick tires for adventure racing. Semi-slick tires provide a low rolling resistance for those times when you will be riding on paved surfaces, and they still provide adequate "grip" for the sections of the race that will be on trail or dirt road.

If you are interested in "upgrading" your existing bike for adventure racing, the best way to improve on what you already have is to purchase a set of lightweight wheels. Wheel weight has a big effect on the speed and acceleration of your bike. Using ultra-lightweight inner tubes is another way to decrease weight.

BRAKES

The advent of V-brakes revolutionized mountain biking by allowing better braking capability. The V-brake is currently the type of braking system that you will find on most new mountain bikes. Disc brakes are making their way into the market now and have the advantage of being able to handle extreme conditions. In muddy riding conditions, the V-brake tends to clog up, making it impossible to ride. The disc brake allows you to ride in muddy conditions. Because almost all adventure races will include riding in mud, the disc brake is starting to show up on more adventure racers' bikes. The brake system is still a matter of the amount of money you are willing to spend—for most adventure races the V-brake system is more than adequate.

Muddy riding will quickly wear down the brake pads on a bike, so be prepared to change your brake pads during a wet and muddy race.

PEDAL SYSTEMS

Most adventure race competitors use a clipless pedal system. The advantages in pedal power far outweigh any potential disadvantages. The use of clipless pedals does, however, necessitate the use of special shoes for the bike sections of the race. This can mean that it will be necessary to then carry your bike shoes with you on, for example, a running section to the bike transition. Also, you may have to hop off your bike and "hike" in these shoes, which may be tricky at best. Some competitors avoid this problem by using toe straps on their bikes that allow them to wear a hiking/running shoe.

The Raid Gauloises 2000 in Tibet started with a short run up and over a steep and rocky pass to the waiting bikes. The bikes had been moved to the transition area the day before the start of the race, and no other gear could be left with the bikes. In addition, after the start of the race, no gear could be left at the bike transition after the run; therefore, all of the competitors with clipless pedal systems had to either carry their bike shoes on the run and their running shoes on the bike or do the run in their bike shoes. Most competitors elected to do the run in their bike shoes. One of our teammates chose to wear an old pair of extra running shoes and carry her bike shoes. At the bike transition, she gave the running shoes to a startled Tibetan who was watching the race, so she wouldn't have to carry them on the bike leg.

Select a pedal system that you are comfortable riding with and that will shed mud easily. We used the Time pedal for the Eco-Challenge 2000 in Borneo because we anticipated a lot of muddy riding—and it worked well. Pedals exist that have a small amount of rotation, or "float," built in to prevent knee stress on the long rides typical of adventure races. If you will be riding in muddy, snowy conditions, spray your cleats and clipless pedals lightly with lube to help keep the snow and mud from sticking to—and clogging—your pedal system.

Platform pedals also exist that work well with a running-type shoe. The biggest consideration is the length of time you are likely to be biking. For the shorter races a system that does not require you to change shoes could be a big advantage. For the longer races, where you could be biking anywhere from 35 to 100 miles at one time, stick with the clipless pedal if you are used to it, and find a comfortable bike shoe.

BIKE SEAT

The greatest number of complaints from beginning racers relates to how sore they get after sitting on their bike saddle for many hours during a race. The solution is simple: Pick a very comfortable seat, even at the sacrifice of weight. You could be on your bike for a very long time!

Most riders like to have the seat level, although a slight nose-down tilt to the saddle can help to reduce pressure. To adjust the level of the seat, try riding with no hands or light pressure on the handlebars. If you slide forward too easily, adjust the tilt back slightly. Too much forward tilt can lead to uncomfortable pressure on the arms and hands, especially with a heavy backpack.

HELMET

We are advocates of wearing a bike helmet at all times—when racing, training, and even when just on a jaunt around the neighborhood or to the grocery store. Adventure races everywhere require that racers wear approved helmets at all times when on the bike. During the Eco-Challenge, the conditions were so hot and humid that when teams were walking with their bikes, many racers took their helmets off to cool down a bit, but they were required to put them on again when on the bike.

Some adventure races are allowing the use of helmets other than approved bike helmets for the bike sections. The lightweight Petzel Meteor, a rock-climbing helmet, is an example of this type of helmet. Conversely, the bike helmet is often approved for the climbing sections.

Before the race, try your headlamp with your helmet if you plan to wear your headlamp during the night bike sections. Some helmets are comfortable with the light under it, or you can attach the light to the outside of your helmet using Velcro or climbing helmet clips (available at mountaineering shops).

Find a method that allows you to quickly and easily attach your head-lamp to your helmet and one that will keep your headlamp on when you are bumping down the trail. There is nothing more annoying than a light that keeps popping off of your helmet or falling in your eyes while you are riding. Test the system before the race and have it ready to go.

LIGHTING SYSTEMS

One crucial race accessory, and a mandatory piece of equipment for a night-time race, is the lighting system the team uses. It is not necessary for each team member to have the same lighting system. However, the advantage of using the same system is that everyone is carrying the same-size replacement batteries during the race and in their gear box at the TA.

Choose a system that will provide you with enough light to ride confi-dently. A five- or ten-watt bulb in, for example, a small NiteRider Sport will light the road or trail sufficiently to allow you to ride closer to your daytime pace. The level of illumination will allow you to spot things before it is too late. Unfortunately, this system requires the use of five D cell batteries, which is rather heavy, and the burn time is generally only six to seven hours. To augment the system and make it last through the night, many racers will also wear their head-lamp, turning off the brighter system when the extra illumination is not required. Remember, a headlamp will throw light wherever you look; a system attached to your handlebars will shine only where the handlebars are pointed.

Many competitors use a low-tech simple setup including an inexpensive light that may run on two C batteries mounted on the front combined with a headlamp. For the best terrain differentiation, it is important to have the light as far away from the eyes as possible, and at an angle to create shadows to distin-guish rocks, holes, and roots. For most races, you shouldn't rely on just a head-lamp for the biking sections. It is a great idea to practice with several systems to see what you like the best and find what gives you the confidence to ride well at night. The farther ahead you can see, the faster you will be able to travel. (To read more about lighting systems, see Chapter 12, "Into the Night.")

TOOLS

Naturally you and your team want to travel as light as possible and eliminate duplication wherever you can. With that in mind look at what each team member already has for bike repair and then select the smallest, lightest option of each and assemble a team bike repair kit for one person to carry on their bike. Depending on the race and the expected terrain, you might decide that it is best for everyone to carry at least one bike tube, and perhaps several. A small and efficient bike pump is important to speed up the repair time. Make sure that everyone on the team uses the same type of tube (either Schrader or Presta valve). If they don't, the team will need to carry a pump that can handle both types of valves, as well as appropriate replacement tubes.

Items to include in the tool kit:

Extra chain links

Chain breaker

Tubes

Patches (self-sticking)

Pump

Lube (if conditions warrant)

Extra spokes and spoke tool

Someone on the team must know how to fix flat tires and broken chains and be able to adjust brakes, spokes, and gears. Carrying the tools will not do you any good if no one can use them.

BIKE ACCESSORIES

Some races require a team odometer, but even if they don't, it is beneficial to have at least one odometer secured on one team member's bike. The odometer can be an invaluable tool to tell you how far you've gone and to alert you to upcoming navigation points. For example, the team navigator might ask the team member with the odometer to let him/her know when the team has traveled a certain distance, so that the team can then begin looking for an important turn. Get comfortable using the odometer in metric and nonmetric modes if you ever think you might race in a country other than the United States.

In one race, for kicks, we attached children's squeeze horns to our bikes. Interestingly, they became very useful when we found ourselves riding a steep downhill section at night. The person in the back was able to signal in case of trouble or just to get the rest of the team to slow down.

CLOTHING

Probably the most important piece of biking equipment, next to the bike itself, is the bike shoe. You can count on walking with your bike for a long period of time during many adventure races. As a result, the shoes you select need to be very comfortable, not only for riding but for walking (usually uphill through water and mud). Most adventure racers use a clipless pedal system, so the shoes they wear have "cleats" on the bottom. Bike shoes are not usually designed for hiking up hills, so pick the most comfortable pair of shoes you can find. The bike shoe industry is beginning to make shoes specifically for adventure racing, understanding that riders will have to hike with their bikes on a portion of the bike section.

Wearing bike shorts during the bike section of a race is a matter of comfort and preference. In the expedition-length races, most competitors take the time to change, knowing that in the long run it is worth it, due to the extra padding it provides for riding in the saddle. In the sprint adventure races, most competitors do the entire race in their bike shorts, so selecting a breathable, fast-drying, and comfortable pair is important.

Carry a lightweight rain-resistant jacket and pants with you on the bike. You are more susceptible to hypothermia during a bike ride, so take precautions to stay dry and warm. The use of gloves in races is purely personal. However, if the weather gets cold, or if there is a significant amount of rocky downhill riding expected, wearing full-fingered leather-palmed bike gloves can be a big help. It could prevent a team member from being unable to paddle in a critical section later in the race due to severely scraped hands. Also, the padding in the bike gloves can help to prevent numbness and tingling in the hands.

TRAVELING TO THE RACE WITH YOUR BIKE

Sooner or later you will find yourself flying with your bike to a race. You might want to invest in a bike case, or find one to borrow. If you choose to buy one, look for a large enough case that will hold extra race gear and will require minimal breakdown of the bike. Some of the larger and longer races (the Eco-Challenge, in particular) require you to unpack and assemble and repack your bike several times during the race. The ability to pack extra items in your bike case comes in handy when the amount of gear you are carrying on an airplane exceeds the weight limit. You can throw some things in with your bike to redistribute the weight—as long as you don't exceed the allowed bike weight. Bike cases with wheels make things much easier if you must fly with your bike.

Be prepared to pay to travel on the airlines with your bike. For example, the fee to travel with your bike domestically on United Airlines is approximately $75 each way. International carriers often consider the bike as a piece of regular luggage, so if you do not exceed the allowable number of bags, there may be no additional fee for traveling with a bike.

TOWING AND OTHER FORMS OF ASSISTANCE

Teams utilize a wide variety of techniques to assist the slower team members or those who are struggling through a bike section. These include towing and pushing while on the bike. A bike towing system can be as simple as a bungee cord attached to the seat post of the towing bike and the handlebar of the bike being towed, or it can be more elaborate and efficient.

A simple bike towing system might consist of a bungee cord or piece of surgical tubing attached under the seat of the towing bike and to the handlebar of the bike being towed. The tubing can be tied to the rails under the seat of the

Getting a push from a teammate.
© 2000 Phil Mislinski

A SAMPLE TOWING SYSTEM

There are many different ways of making and attaching a towing system. One way is to:

1. Cut a piece of small diameter rigid plastic tubing so that it measures from the nose of the saddle to a few inches beyond the end of the rear wheel, or use the top section of a fishing pole.

2. Thread surgical tubing through the plastic tubing or fishing pole.

3. Attach one end of the surgical tubing to the rails beneath the seat.

4. Secure the plastic tube or fishing pole between the rails under the seat using zip ties or other means.

5. Place a large loop in the other end of the surgical tubing (so that it will hang off of the back of the bike).

6. Make sure that the surgical tubing is not long enough to get tangled in the rear wheel.

7. Attach a hook onto the handle bar of the bike to be towed. For example, use a bike pump holder piece (the kind that fits on the top tube and has the small raised nipple).

8. To use the system, the person needing to be towed rides up behind and to the side of the bike with the towing system, grabs the dangling loop, and places it over the hook on the handlebar.

Using a towing system on the bike.
© 1999 Darrin Eisman

towing bike, and a small loop with a small light carabiner can be attached to the other end. When the system is not being used, it can be hooked under the seat of the towing bike.

A more elaborate system can be devised that allows the tubing to remain in place, extended out over the end of the towing bike's wheel so that the person needing the tow can easily ride up behind the towing bike, grab onto the tubing, and hook it onto their handlebar. A rigid piece of PVC tubing or a piece of a fishing pole can be used to thread the flexible surgical tubing through so that when the towing system is not in use the surgical tubing will not fall and get tangled in the rear wheel of the towing bike.

Another method of providing assistance to a rider is to ride beside them with a hand on their back or on their backpack. Even a very slight push while riding can help a struggling teammate tremendously. Alternatively, practice riding next to a teammate while holding on to a strap on their pack or shirt, or whatever you can grab to get a quick "tow."

There are some tricks you can practice to improve your riding and increase your overall comfort during an adventure race. Don't grip the handlebars too tightly while riding—lightly tap or drum your fingers on the handlebar now and then to remind yourself to stay loose. Occasionally take a hand completely off of the handlebar and shake it to relax your shoulder and elbow and get the blood moving to the hand to prevent numbness. Change your body position frequently to prevent fatigue, and when riding on easy terrain, take the time to stretch out the back and legs while on the bike.

Sooner or later you will encounter unrideable sections of an adventure race where you will be required to walk your bike. During these hike-a-bike sections, work together as a team and keep moving. Have a stronger team member take a second bike so that they are pushing two up the hill, allowing the other teammate to walk unencumbered and swiftly up the hill.

Remember—sometimes it is just as efficient and less of an energy drain

Hike-a-bike at Eco-Challenge 2000.
© 2000 Dan Campbell

to walk your bike up a hill. Learn to unclip either foot quickly. Putting the left foot down when stopping might help to prevent a chain ring tattoo on the right calf.

Most of us do not ride with a heavy pack on our back during our recreational rides. Therefore, it is important to practice doing this because the added weight will slow you down and increases the effort you put out dramatically. In addition, the weight can affect your balance when riding single-track trails. Choose a pack with a waistband that you can put food in so that you have easy access during the rides, or attach a small bag to the handlebars for quick access.

Adventure races will have you riding through all kinds of conditions, especially mud. To ride through mud, remember to shift into a lower gear, slide back on the saddle, and keep your momentum up. Try to pick a straight line through the muddy section—don't turn—and then just power through.

Adventure races will take a toll on your bike. It is likely that by the end of the race you have ridden through sand, mud, and water. Take the time to clean your bike, examine all parts, and lube it before you begin training for your next race.

CHAPTER 6

PADDLING

© 1998 Dan Campbell

This chapter is meant to familiar- ize the beginning adventure racer with the sport of paddling. The best advice is to get edu- cated, get equipped, get trained, and then get on the water—a lot.

Adventure races typically involve a significant amount of paddling. This can be in canoes or kayaks on moving rivers; in rafts on big whitewater; and canoes and kayaks on flat water such as lakes, reservoirs, and oceans.

Whitewater refers to moving bodies of water like rivers, streams, and brooks. The river current interacts with the river features (rocks, sudden drops) to form interesting and challenging water features like eddies, waves, and holes. Moving water is rated as to challenge and difficulty—ranging from Class I to Class VI. Class I and Class II waters are generally easy and straightforward to navigate, with wide clear channels negotiable by most novice paddlers. Class III water is intermediate in nature, with waves that are difficult to avoid. Complex maneuvers may be required in tight passages or around ledges and where strong eddies can be found. Class IV and V rapids are for more advanced boaters and require precise boat handling. Class VI waters are considered unnegotiable for all but the extreme boater.

Most adventure races will include a mix of flat-water paddling and white- water travel. Class I and Class II moving waters are common in adventure racing, along with an occasional Class III rapid. These will be negotiated either by canoe (inflatable or hard side) or kayak. If a river included in an adventure race contains Class IV rapids, it will most likely be run in a raft. Many adventure races will provide a guide in the raft for the entire section or, at a minimum, for the trickiest rapids in

Team Sierra Nevada in the rapids of Rio Manso at Eco-Challenge 1999 in Argentina.
© 1999 Dan Campbell

the section. Often the racers will be required to "scout" a rapid if it is difficult or the least bit dangerous. "Scouting" means that each team is required to pull the boat to the shore above the rapid and one or all team members will get out and view the rapid to determine the safest line through before attempting to run it. Many races will have signs posted above a rapid indicating the best line through.

A general rule of thumb in adventure racing is that roughly one-quarter of the time of the entire race will be spent in a boat. In a short five-to-eight-hour race you should be prepared to paddle for at least two hours. This could be a single two-hour paddle or be broken up into several shorter paddle sections, depending on the specific racecourse. In a race lasting twenty-four to thirty-six hours, you could have a single paddle section of up to ten-plus hours. This is also true in a three-to-five-day race, but instead of one ten-hour paddle you will have several long paddle sections.

For safety reasons it is typical for the moving water sections of an adventure race to be designated as dark zones. Competitors will not be allowed to start a water section after a certain time of day (usually sundown) and will not be allowed to start the water section until daylight. This usually applies to river sections with rapids and hazards such as rocks and submerged trees. In the longer races it is incumbent on the competitors to stop along the river and wait until the designated time to get back on the water. This often provides an excellent opportunity for the team to catch up on some sleep in the middle of the race.

EQUIPMENT

Paddling equipment that a racer may be required to bring to the race can include:

Boat (although usually provided)

Paddles

Personal flotation device (PFD, such as a life jacket)

Helmet

Wetsuit

Safety throw bag

Bailer or pump

Dry bag

BOATS

Most, but not all, adventure races will provide each team with boats. This might be hard-sided canoes, inflatable canoes, or kayaks. If rafting is included in the race, rafts will typically be provided. In expedition-length races such as the ELF or the Eco-Challenge, special indigenous boats might be provided. For example, in the Eco-Challenge 2000, perahu outrigger sailboats and wooden sampan canoes unique to the area were specially made for competitors to use in the race.

Kayaks are narrow boats that sit low in the water, usually entirely closed over with decking, except for an opening where the racer sits (or multiple openings for more than one racer). Sit-on-top kayaks, which can also be used in adventure races, are similar in design, but with no enclosed decking—the paddler simply sits on top of the kayak. The most common type of kayak used in adventure races is the touring, or sea, kayak suited to flat water and ocean paddling. Contemporary hard-sided kayaks are made of either fiberglass or polyethylene plastic, or a combination of materials, such as Kevlar and fiberglass. Plastic boats are most often used in adventure races because they are virtually indestructible. However, they tend to weigh more than boats made of fiberglass or Kevlar.

A two-person kayak is often referred to as a K-2; a four-person kayak is a K-4, and so on. Kayaks are paddled with a two-bladed paddle. The kayaker sits with legs stretched forward to the bow of the kayak, with the knees snugly nestled against the underside of the deck. A "spray skirt" or "spray deck" may be

FOREIGN PADDLING LINGO

For those racing in foreign countries, river travel is often referred to as "navigation." In addition, a "canoe" may be used as a general term to include both kayaks and what we know of as canoes in the United States. Often the term "Canadian canoe" will be used to distinguish a canoe from a kayak.

used to cover the opening, with the kayaker seated in the boat. It is a garment that fits snugly around the kayaker's waist and torso, then flares out to fit snugly around the rim of the opening of the boat, keeping water out of the boat. If a kayaker flips the boat over while using a spray skirt, they can either roll the kayak back upright using the paddle and the hips if they know how, or do a "wet exit" and get out of the boat. Every adventure racer should at least know how to comfortably and quickly do a wet exit from a kayak.

Hard-sided canoes are similar to kayaks except for the positioning of the paddlers. The seats are higher and the paddlers sit either on their knees, with their buttocks resting on the seat for maximum power and stability, or directly on the canoe seat for endurance paddles. The interior of the boat remains open, so water can freely enter over the rim, making it necessary to keep a bailing device handy. It is important to attach the bailer and any other loose items in the boat so they will not be lost if the boat capsizes.

Rafting the whitewater at Eco-Challenge 1996.
© 1996 Dan Campbell

Inflatable kayaks and canoes are popular in adventure races. Inflatable canoes can hold a lot of gear and the paddlers are not in enclosed cockpits. These boats are typically forgiving in whitewater, they bounce off rocks, and require very little water to float because they are so buoyant. They are stable boats but can be difficult to steer on flat water. It is possible that each team will be required to inflate their boat or boats prior to use on the water. If possible, you should find an inflatable boat similar to the ones you will be using in the race and practice this so you know how to inflate them quickly and ensure that the valves are closed.

Rafts are inflatable craft that are paddled by several people using single-bladed paddles. They are typically between 12 and 18 feet long and are much more stable than kayaks and canoes but less maneuverable. They are used in more difficult moving water and require boating knowledge and experience.

PADDLES

Paddles may or may not be provided by the race organizers. Often each team is allowed to determine what type of paddle to use in the race. Two types of paddles are typically used: canoe paddles (for canoeing and rafting) and kayak paddles (for canoeing and kayaking). When determining the best paddle to use in a race, consider the weight of the material and the blade shape and whether you will be required to carry the paddles to the boating section.

Kayak paddles are either flat or feathered. "Feathered" means that the blades are offset at an angle, between 70 and 90 degrees. The benefit is that while one blade is in the water the other is at a flat angle to the wind so that it doesn't act as a mini-sail and blow you off course. Kayak blades are either flat or "spooned." A spooned blade takes a more powerful bite of the water but can take some getting used to. For adventure racing look for kayak paddles that come apart in the middle so that the feather offset can be changed if desired and so that transport is easier. Lightweight carbon fiber paddles are popular for endurance paddling.

Adventure racers typically use kayak paddles for canoeing. You have more blade time in the water with a kayak paddle because the opposing blade is already most of the way through its recovery stroke while the other blade is still in the water.

HYDRO-SPEED

A relatively new sport, hydro-speed, is making an appearance in adventure races. Hydro-speed, or whitewater swimming, is popular in Europe and involves an individual lying on their stomach on a "boogie-type" board while negotiating the whitewater. Protective gear, such as knee and thigh pads, wetsuits, and helmets, is important for this event.

PERSONAL FLOATATION DEVICE (PFD)

PFDs are most often required gear for an adventure race that involves paddling and/or whitewater swimming. Look for one with minimal obstruction to your paddling stroke and with a food pocket in the front. Make sure that the vest fits so that it won't chafe, or wear appropriate clothing underneath to prevent rubbing on bare skin.

Additional PFD attachments required by many adventure races include a river knife and whistle. A rescue knife attached to the PFD can be life saving in the event that you get trapped underwater and need to cut yourself free (or a teammate can cut the rope, branch, or whatever is holding you). An example of the usefulness of the knife occurred in an endurance race in Colorado when one team's inflatable canoe flipped and trapped one of the competitors underneath. River safety personnel used a knife to slash and deflate the inflatable canoe and release the trapped competitor. A whistle can be used to quickly get someone's attention in an emergency.

HELMET

A paddling helmet should provide coverage of the forehead, temples, and ears. For many adventure races where teams will only be encountering Class I and Class II water, the use of a bike or climbing helmet is allowed for the water sections.

WETSUIT

A wetsuit is an outfit made of neoprene rubber 2 to 5 millimeters thick for paddling. It works by providing a layer of insulation and by trapping a thin layer of water between your body and the wetsuit. This layer of water is easily warmed by your body and keeps you warm. A dry suit is a waterproof nylon outfit, loosely fitting, with latex rubber gaskets at the neck, wrists, and ankles, with a waterproof zipper. It is worn over standard insulating clothing. Drysuits can also be made of Gore-Tex.

SAFETY THROW BAG

A safety throw bag consists of a minimum of 15 meters of buoyant rope carried in a small pouch. The purpose of the bag is to throw it to people who are out of their boats and swimming; they grab on to the bag, the thrower digs in and holds the end of the rope tightly, and the current pushes the swimmer to the side of the river rather than carrying them downstream.

Never tie a bag to yourself in whitewater, and if the throw bag is attached to something in the boat (a good idea in case you flip), make sure you have a way to release it quickly. A very small, light carabiner can be used to attach the throw rope to the boat. Many commercial throw bags are constructed of heavy-duty materials and weigh more than 2 pounds. This is no problem unless you have to carry the throw bag and all of your river equipment on a hike or bike section to the boats. Look for (or make) a small, lightweight throw bag, containing approximately 20 to 25 meters of 8-millimeter polyethylene rope.

BAILER OR PUMP

While traveling on whitewater or flat water with waves, you will get wet and the boat will begin to take on water—even if you don't capsize. A water bailer or pump is a necessary item to have in each boat. Even a small amount of water collected in the boat can decrease the maneuverability of the boat substantially. Remember—each gallon of water weighs 8 pounds!

A simple bailer made by cutting the bottom end off of a large bleach bottle or an orange juice or milk jug (something with a handle) is sufficient for most cases. An inexpensive hand pump, available at any river boating store, is a good investment and removes a large volume of water quickly from a boat.

DRY BAG

Dry bags come in many sizes and are designed to keep gear and clothing dry. They are made of sealable rubberized sacks with a top that rolls down tightly and fastens. Some dry bags come with straps so that they can be worn as a backpack, which can come in handy in an adventure race where you have to carry your gear to the boat section.

Tips for packing your gear and clothing within the dry bag:

▲ Use many little "bags within the bag" to organize and isolate your gear, and to provide an additional waterproof layer.

▲ Place clothing, food, and safety gear in heavy Ziploc bags, separated so that you can easily grab what you need.

▲ If you will be boating where you know everything will get very wet, use two Ziploc bags, one inside the other, to protect your food, clothing, and other belongings.

▲ Place the items you will need quickly near the top so you aren't digging through the dry bag to find food.

LONG-DISTANCE PADDLING TECHNIQUES

It is crucial to get good instruction on paddling in order to learn to do it right. Paddling correctly can make the difference between a comfortable long paddle and a stressful and fatiguing long paddle. Some general things to keep in mind for adventure race paddling are:

▲ Make every stroke a forward stroke to preserve your forward momentum.

▲ Keep your arms as straight as possible to ensure using the large muscles of your back and torso.

▲ Use the big muscles of your back and trunk, which don't fatigue as quickly as the arms, by rotating the trunk at each stroke.

▲ Use proper hand placement on the paddle—hold the paddle over your head with your elbows shoulder height and make sure the elbows and forearms create a 90-degree angle with the paddle.

Team Vail portaging their kayaks.
©1999 Dan Campbell

▲ Remove the paddle from the water when the stroke reaches your hip to prevent wasted motion and effort.

▲ When learning, watch the blade as it strokes through the water—this forces your body to rotate properly.

▲ Get instruction.

▲ Practice, practice, practice.

The secret to stroke efficiency and comfort for endurance paddling is trunk rotation. This conserves energy and uses the stronger muscles of the back; using the arms alone will tire you very quickly.

In a two-person boat, the person in the back (stern) of the boat makes corrective strokes to keep the boat going straight. The more experienced paddler can make small corrections with a minimum loss of forward speed. This is particularly important in adventure racing or any paddling race against the clock. Get instruction on the correct minimalist strokes and then practice them. There is nothing more frustrating than having your boat go in circles or weave its way across a lake while other teams are taking a direct line.

When two team members will be in one boat, consideration to weight distribution and paddling ability must be given. The more experienced paddler will generally be placed in the back of the boat and the stronger people will be placed in the front. The front person provides the power and is not responsible for the direction that the boat travels. Communication between paddlers is critical and teamwork is essential so that everyone knows what they are supposed to do.

DRINKING AND EATING WHILE PADDLING

Two of the hardest things to do while paddling are eating and drinking, because your arms are busy! If you stop to eat or drink, the boat could drift and your forward momentum will be halted. Find ways to ensure that you are continuing to take in fluids and food. Food needs to be readily accessible in pockets on your PFD and in double Ziploc bags within reach (double bagged because it will get wet!). A mesh sleeve to hold your hydration bladder can be sewn onto your PDF. Attach stiff plastic tubing that fits around your neck to your hydration tube so that you can drink "hands free."

OTHER CLOTHING
CONSIDERATIONS

FOOTWEAR

In an adventure race, competitors usually will wear their running shoes in the boat, removing them if there is an opportunity to dry out the feet while paddling. Another typical type of footwear is a river sandal or river shoe, created specifically for boating. It is often necessary to portage, or carry, your boat in an adventure race, so wear something on your feet that you feel comfortable walking in, with a good sole made for walking on slippery rock surfaces.

If the water is particularly cold, neoprene booties could be the best thing to wear on your feet to keep them warm. Seal Skinz socks or neoprene socks can also be worn.

SPRAY JACKET

Spray jackets, also known as paddling jackets, are a good layering option when you know you will be getting wet. These jackets are made of treated nylon. Pull the jacket over the head and fasten around the neck, sleeves, and waist with neoprene and Velcro closures. If you don't have a spray jacket, wear a rain jacket or shell to help keep you dry.

GLOVES

Water-softened hands are prone to blistering, especially over the long periods of paddling time that can occur in an adventure race. A simple paddling glove or bike glove can help to prevent blistering. A special glove such as Seal Skinz can keep your hands dry and warm.

Another option is a pogie, a "mitten," that straps to the paddle shaft. Your hand slips into the pogie so you can hold the paddle but still be protected from the elements. These are great for training in cold weather.

SAILING AWAY

Sails and kites can be used in races to make the boat go faster. In the Eco-Challenge 2000, one team had extensively practiced flying a kite that would catch the winds and increase their boat speed. They were able to travel significantly faster than any other boat in the race. Sails act as spinnakers to catch the wind when it is coming from behind you. They can be made from almost anything—simply holding up a jacket to catch the wind can help.

CHAPTER 7

TREKKING

Mountain trekking in Morocco.
© 1998 Dan Campbell

Every adventure race will keep you on your feet for an extended period of time. Whether it's a sprint race that takes three to ten hours, or the Eco-Challenge, the time spent trekking will constitute a significant percentage of the overall duration of the event (easily 25 to 35 percent). The term "trekking," for purposes within the sport of adventure racing, refers to running, hiking, or otherwise moving forward on your feet. In events of twenty-four hours or less, winning teams will actually run most of these sections. In longer races, generally, these teams will run the downhills and some flat sections. Beginner teams are more likely to walk or trek at a comfortable, fast pace throughout the race, with little if any running.

Webster's New Collegiate Dictionary defines trekking as "to go on an arduous journey." We like this definition. Not only is trekking a physically demanding component of any adventure race, it is also a mental challenge. Pacing is extremely important so as to not expend too much energy early on and "crash and burn" later (though this is true for all disciplines). At times, however, teams will want to pick up the pace and push harder to either beat a dark zone or to pass another team and beat them to a section where there may be a wait (like a ropes section). Teams must also recognize the different levels of ability among the team members, and trek at a pace suitable for all. Many times, therefore, teams will have a slower teammate lead the trek. The most important mental aspect to trekking, however, is its navigation component. Teams can expect trekking to provide the greatest opportunity for navigation and choices of direction in a race and, thus, the greatest opportunity to gain time or, possibly, get lost.

What kind of terrain can one expect in an adventure race? Virtually anything other than a flat paved surface. Races may take place in jungles, mountains, forests, deserts, canyons, and marshes. Race directors definitely look for a variety of nontraditional and challenging terrain for competitors to travel over. One can certainly expect lots of uphill and downhill, trails, deadfall, rocks, ridges, drainages, and forest. It is also fairly common to traverse on the side of a hill or slope and, therefore, it is advisable to train on this and other varied terrain

NEVER GIVE UP

In the Expedition Mata Atlantica 1999 in Brazil, our team found itself essentially lost in the jungle trekking for nearly twenty hours. We spent most of that time with two other equally lost teams (who we got to know very well), all trying to work together to exit the jungle in the right place. After a full day and night, we finally came upon what we thought was the village with the checkpoint we were looking for; however, it turned out we were still nearly 10 miles away from the correct village. Frustrated and tired, we found a little café where we drank colas and grape fanta and ate pizza. Convinced we were pretty much out of the race, having been lost for so long, we took our time and ultimately began our trek toward the checkpoint. About halfway there, a helicopter spotted us and, almost immediately, anxious and excited race officials and media besieged us. Before one of the teams we were traveling with was able to say they wanted to withdraw from the race, we were informed that more than twenty teams were still in the jungle, and our three teams were in ninth, tenth, and eleventh place! Moral of the story? Never ever give up!

to improve one's confidence, ability, balance, and strength.

Because of its inherently slower pace, trekking provides an opportunity to talk with your teammates, occasionally travel with other teams and get to know them, and interact with the people who live in the area. Once again, during the EMA 1999 in Brazil, while trekking, we came across a family living high and isolated in the mountains. They did not speak English (and we did not speak Portuguese) but offered us coffee and bananas and looked at our map while we tried to ask them how to get where we wanted to go. Finally, one of the men grabbed a machete, signaled to follow him, and proceeded to lead us on our way.

While trekking in an adventure race, it is likely that the team will cross many streams and rivers. This can be a dangerous undertaking in some circumstances and requires knowledge of water to choose the best place to cross. Water usually moves the fastest at its narrowest point. Sometimes, crossing where the water is wider and deeper can be easier to trek through. For any deep or swift stream or river crossing:

▲ Unfasten the straps on your backpack so you can remove it in case it gets caught on something.

▲ If traveling with trekking poles, use them to provide balance, or find a big stick to use.

▲ Keep your shoes on to protect your feet and prevent slipping.

▲ Move slowly and deliberately, planting your feet firmly.

Never move across swift water while tied to a rope. If you slip, fall, and go under, it is possible that you will become trapped underwater because of the rope. Linking arms with your teammates, or holding onto and stabilizing a teammate while crossing, is often a worthwhile teamwork effort.

TREAD LIGHTLY

In adventure racing, there is an effort to remain environmentally friendly, and nowhere is this more evident than in the trekking sections. Race directors enforce a "Leave No Trace" or "Tread Lightly" policy, requiring all competitors to pack out what they pack in, and not leave litter behind. In some cases, this can also include packing out human waste. How can a team minimize its impact on the environment while traveling through an area? If an existing trail is available, travel single file on it; conversely, if the team goes off trail, spread out across from each other as you trek so that you aren't impacting a single area.

Each discipline within an adventure race requires different gear and clothing considerations. Let's examine some of these relative to trekking.

BACKPACKS

One major difference between adventure racing and other sports such as running, biking, or triathlon is the presence of a backpack on your back at all times (though a fanny or hydration pack may suffice in sprint events). The backpack is necessary to carry water, food, extra clothing, and various gear required by race management typically for safety purposes. Running or trekking with a backpack is very different than without. It is absolutely essential to train as much as possible

Salomon X-Adventure in Aspen, Colorado.
© 2000 Salomon N.A./Thomas Zuccareno

with a backpack on. As you become accustomed and comfortable with this, adding weight to the pack will best help you prepare for the real thing. It is not uncommon to carry 20 to 25 pounds or more in your pack during a longer event (12 to 18 pounds in shorter events). Water is a big factor in the weight of your pack, and this is largely dependent on how long the section is and how often you anticipate being able to replenish your water supply. We recommend using a water reservoir ("bladder") as often as possible during training to further prepare for the actual race (while adding weight to your pack).

There are several features to look for in a good backpack for adventure racing. In fact, several manufacturers have now designed backpacks specifically with an eye toward adventure racing. As you should always look to minimize weight with all gear, look for the lightest, most workable and comfortable pack you can find. There are many packs with a 30-liter capacity that are less than 2 pounds. Food pockets on the waist belt allow you to access food while racing without having to slow down or stop. Exterior mesh pockets serve a similar purpose, allowing storage of food or extra clothing that a teammate may also readily access without having to stop. Remember: A key to successful adventure racing is continuous forward progress (minimize stopping!).

An internal hydration bladder pocket is a handy feature, segregating and nicely fitting your bladder away from other gear in your pack. When refilling your bladder, it is common to get it wet; therefore, keeping it away from (hopefully) dry clothes and food in your pack is advisable. If the pack does not have an internal pocket for the bladder, it is simply placed in the main compartment.

A chest strap is also a good backpack feature, as it better secures the pack to your body, thus minimizing movement as you trek. Most important, though, are overall fit and comfort, when selecting your backpack. Find one that fits your body well, with comfortable shoulder straps, a waist belt that sits nicely and firmly on your hips, and one that fits your torso properly. Many packs seem designed for a longer, typically male torso; women or less tall people need to be especially alert to this.

Most backpacks come with added straps and other features that add weight and bulk. Examine these to see if they are things you will use and, if not, consider cutting them off. Don't be afraid to alter your pack to fit your needs—add an extra mesh compartment to the top of the pack, for example, if you love the pack but just feel it needs some extra storage space. Some packs come equipped to carry bottles on the shoulder straps for easy access. Elastic cord and quick-locks can be attached to the shoulder strap on any pack to alter it to carry water bottles.

Easy-access water bottle on the shoulder strap of a backpack.
© 2000 Phil Mislinski

FOOTWEAR

Together with the backpack, probably the other most important piece of gear for trekking is the shoe. It seems that the most common injury affecting adventure racers are blisters on the feet. In Eco-Challenge 2000 John Howard—considered by most as the world's best adventure racer—was forced out of the race with terrible blister and foot problems, as were many other racers and teams. This particular race was made even more difficult due to competitors' feet being wet throughout the race, as well as trekking and sliding through vast amounts of mud in the jungle. Good footwear and socks will go a long way toward blister prevention and foot protection.

Jungle trekking during the Eco-Challenge 2000 in Borneo.
© 2000 Barry Siff

More and more shoe companies are following the lead of Salomon and their popular Raid Wind shoe in bringing specific shoes for adventure racing to the market. However, a large number of racers simply use a solid trail running shoe and find this quite satisfactory. Beyond the number-one criteria of pure comfort when selecting a shoe, consider that rocks and water will be commonplace in most any adventure race. Therefore, look for a shoe that will expel water, as well as one with a very solid rubber sole and "toe guard" in the front to protect you from hitting a rock head-on (this is just a rubber extension of the sole). A good shoe will also fit well around the ankle, helping to prevent pebbles and other debris from getting inside. The Raid Wind has all these features plus a purposeful quick and "expandable" lacing system. It utilizes a cord and quick-lock system, which eliminates the need to tie the shoes, and includes a place to "hide" the quick-lock so you can easily put on and remove the shoe, as necessary. The lacing system also allows you to loosen or enlarge the shoe gradually as your feet swell during a race, as they are prone to do. Because feet tend to swell, it is advisable to race in a shoe generally one full size larger than normal.

Some shoes are now designed with detachable ankle-high gaiters, which help seal the ankle area. In the absence of such, and when racing in snow, sand, mud, or dirt conditions, many racers will wear separate gaiters, protecting their shins and helping keep debris out of their shoes. Gaiters attach securely on and under the shoe, as well as around the ankle, calf, or shin. They come in various sizes and materials, which will affect how much of your leg is covered and how hot (or warming in cool weather) the gaiter will be. The strap that attaches to the gaiter and secures on the underside of your shoe will receive much wear and abuse during a race. Rather than the normal lace or cord that may come with the gaiter, we replace it with a stronger, more durable piece of metal cord or wire, crimped to hold it in place. This will last a lot longer.

Many shoes on the market are lined with Gore-Tex to keep your feet dry in wet conditions. For some races, this may be useful. However, a Gore-Tex liner will not be of any help when you travel through water that goes up over the top of your shoe.

SOCKS

Socks are the "final barrier" for your feet against blisters. As such, sock selection and care during races is extremely important. Blisters are essentially caused by friction against the skin. Minimizing friction on your feet, for that reason, will greatly assist in blister prevention. Many racers use a lubricant for this purpose, such as Hydropel. Our own Team Friction Free had great success in this area in Eco-Challenge 2000 in the jungles of Borneo. Our use of Blister Guard socks, which contain Teflon material in the high blister areas of the heel and toe, provided excellent blister prevention. In fact, Adrian Cohen, Eco-Challenge's medical director, commented that our team "had better feet after the race than at least 90 percent of the field."

While good fit and minimal slide or friction in the socks are key, keeping your feet and socks as dry as possible is equally important. When stopping for a rest, a bite to eat, or a longer transition, take the time to air out your feet and change to a dry pair of socks. These are both great investments toward keeping your feet in good repair. Also, be alert to "hot spots," or developing blisters, and treat them early (more on this in "Injuries and Illnesses," Chapter 14).

Many racers wear Gore-Tex or Seal Skinz socks to keep their feet from getting too wet. The winning team at the ELF Authentic Adventure Race 2000 used the Seal Skinz socks and, in a race where attrition due to the ravages of overly wet feet was a major factor, this turned out to be a great decision by the team.

CLOTHING AND ACCESSORIES

In addition to shoes and socks, other clothing and accessories for trekking include shorts and pants, tops, sunglasses, head coverings, gloves, and sunscreen. Primary consideration for each of these relates to protection of the body and comfort. Generally, in warm- or hot-weather races, clothing should be lightweight, breathable, and quick drying. More and more sport-specific clothing is appearing on the market with excellent materials, unique venting, and other features like drainage holes in the pockets. RailRiders is a good example of this, as some twenty-five teams in the Eco-Challenge 2000 raced in their clothing.

While some people will continue to compete and trek in biking and running shorts, most competitors have turned to looser, lighter clothing in the longer adventure races. In shorter events, however, biking shorts and tighter tops (Lycra, singlets) are often worn throughout, so as to minimize transition time between disciplines. Adventure racers must also consider whether they will be trekking through brush, off-trail, or through jungle, for example, where covering the body is even more of a concern to minimize scrapes and cuts, which can easily become infected. In some cases, you may also consider wearing gloves to protect your hands.

Although more abundant clothing is certainly necessary in cold-weather races, strong consideration must still be given to being lightweight, breathable, and quick drying. Additionally, you should also consider the compactability of your clothing, that is, how well and how small it can be compacted to fit in your backpack (the smaller, the better). The key to traveling comfortably in cold weather is through "layering." This refers to using a few layers of clothing to maintain the comfort you desire. Adding or shedding layers will act as your own thermostat control. While this primarily occurs on your upper body, adding wind or rain pants over tights or shorts has the same effect.

It is particularly important in cold weather that your base layer breathes and pulls away the moisture from your body. To the greatest extent possible, you want to wick any moisture from your body all the way to the exterior of your outer layer of clothing. This will keep you drier and much more comfortable. New technology in clothing accomplishes this extremely well, and we even see "temperature regulation" clothing, which acts like a thermostat in broadening your comfort zone. As Team Outlast in the Raid Gauloises 2000, we used many such pieces of clothing with Outlast—a temperature regulation ingredient—in them. This included socks, gloves, hats, base layer tops, and our waterproof mountaineering jackets. It was very effective, given the wide range of altitude and climates faced in that race in Nepal and Tibet. Fleece and Gore-Tex jackets are oftentimes required gear in races for safety purposes. Be aware, however, that as you move from "water-resistant" to "waterproof," you generally are sacrificing breathability of the material.

Additional clothing to be considered in all kinds of weather includes the use of various head coverings. One extremely versatile piece worn by adventure racers is the Buff. This is a garment, shaped like a tube, that you can use to cover your head (like a "do-rag") and neck, wear as a head or neckband, or use in a number of different ways. They are quite popular among European athletes. At the Raid Gauloises 2000, the days prior to the race were punctuated by high winds and dust, and competitors were camping out at the start line. The Buffs proved to be invaluable for protection against the blowing sand and dirt.

Foreign Legion–type hats are also common in adventure racing in extremely hot conditions. These not only provide sun protection to your head and face, but they have material that extends and covers the back of your neck, which is normally exposed. Sunglasses are sometimes actually required gear; but, in any event, they should be part of your protection from the sun, wind, and debris.

TREKKING ASSISTANCE

Trekking poles are another piece of equipment that many racers will utilize. These add stability while trekking, particularly over rocky surfaces or through stream crossings. They also relieve a notable amount of pressure on your lower back and knees. At least one study has shown that literally tons of pressure is taken off the lower body each hour when using trekking poles. This is most true when going downhill. We use Leki trekking poles that are both light and collapsible. This allows

Trekking in the high
mountains of British
Columbia.
© 1996 Dan Campbell

the user to adjust the length of the poles to one's height and the type of terrain being traveled. When going uphill, poles are shortened; when traveling downhill, they are lengthened. The primary drawback to using trekking poles is having to carry them when not in use, as they can ride awkwardly on or in your pack and potentially get caught on trees or brush.

When it comes to teamwork, there is no place more obvious in most races than during trekking sections. Towing a teammate through the use of a carabineer and surgical tubing or bungee cord is very commonplace in adventure racing. A stronger person (at the time) will greatly assist someone who is suffering or slow at the moment by towing him or her. This is particularly noticeable when going up hills. However, it is equally helpful when running, as the person being towed will literally be pulled through the air as both feet are off the ground in stride. It is definitely worth practicing this and finding a system the team is comfortable with.

Adventure racing is both a thrilling and an arduous journey; as such, trekking is a large component of nearly every adventure race. Being comfortable traveling on your feet for three to eight hours at a time for a weekend or two-day race, or up to two days straight in a race of five days or more is absolutely imperative. In addition, give every consideration to the gear and clothing that you use during this discipline. Weight, comfort, and individual features are critical to analyze and put to your maximum benefit. Teamwork is the key to adventure racing success, and recognizing this before you race and how it may be applied during the trekking—and all other sections—is vital.

CHAPTER 8

MOUNTAINEERING SKILLS

© 1999 Dan Campbell

Mountaineering, or traveling in the mountains, can involve skills such as travel on fixed ropes; traversing across snowfields, ice, and glaciers; and crossing exposed rocks, talus, and scree slopes. Many of these skills are incorporated into adventure races. Simple rope skills are sometimes even included in a sprint-type or twenty-four-hour race. More advanced skills are generally found in the longer, expedition-style races. Longer races have begun to include "canyoneering" as a discipline that utilizes mountaineering skills, including rope work, but it takes place along waterways within canyons.

ROPE TRAVEL

Most adventure races include some form of rope skill. It is important to get training in rope skills before the race from knowledgeable instructors. The most common skills included in races are rappels, ascending on fixed ropes, the Tyrolean traverse, and hiking while clipped to a fixed line.

The rope sections included in adventure races are generally fairly simple, but potentially dangerous, especially when fatigue, anxiety, lack of sleep, or simple lack of training come into play. In an adventure race, the ropes are set up by experienced people and each competitor will be assisted to ensure that personal equipment is properly set up and safety procedures are followed. This, however, does not preclude the need for every competitor to be proficient in performing each of the rope skills required in the race.

MANDATORY ROPE EQUIPMENT

Following is a list of the typical required equipment for rope skills in most races:

> Personal harness
> Climbing helmet (bike helmets
>   are often accepted in races)
> Carabiners
> Prusik safety rope
> Descending device
> Mechanical ascenders
> Foot loop(s)
> Slings or daisy chains

Dramatic 400-foot rappel at Eco-Challenge 1995.
© 1995 Dan Campbell

RAPPELS

In adventure races, rappels (also called abseils) are roped descents using an aluminum alloy or stainless steel descending device such as a Figure 8 or a tube-type belay device (e.g., ATC). Each of these devices provides friction, allowing a controlled descent. The Figure 8 is easy to thread onto the rope and is easy and quick to descend with. Because the Figure 8 has a tendency to cause the rope to twist during the descent and does not dissipate heat very well, many adventure races do not allow them. The tubular-style of descending device can sometimes be difficult to thread, especially if the rope that is being used is fairly thick and new, making it somewhat stiff. One trick to threading the tubular device with stiff, thick rope is to take a small loop and bite it to flatten it out before sticking it through the tube.

Descending devices work by threading the rope through the device, which creates friction to the rope as you descend. Not only is friction created by the rope traveling through the descending device, it can be increased by pulling on the rope with your "brake hand." The brake hand is one hand placed below the descending device in order to control the rate of descent. The brake hand maintains a position on the rope near the hip. Additional friction can be applied to the rope by wrapping the hand around the hip to the back. This action will stop the descent. Under no circumstances should the brake hand be removed from the rope unless the rope has been tied off or secured so that the person cannot descend. If anything happens during the rappel, such as tipping over backward from leaning out too far or having an unbalanced load, use the brake hand to stop and stabilize—do not let go.

On the long rappels typical of an adventure race (up to 150 meters), the weight of the rope adds additional friction and slows the descent, especially at the beginning of the rappel, where it may be necessary to forcefully feed the rope through the descending device by lifting the rope in your brake hand above the descending device and pushing it through. As you go down the rope, it will become easier to descend quickly and smoothly.

The start of the rappel is always the most nerve-wracking. Once over the edge, the rest is easy. Be sure and place the legs nearly perpendicular to the slope to gain stability, lean back to tension the rope, and lower your buttocks. Once over the edge, keep your feet shoulder width apart for stability, look over your shoulder toward the brake hand side to select your footing, lean out away from the rock, and descend smoothly. Bounces and leaps are not safe descending practices—they just look good in the movies!

In a lot of races the rappel will include getting past an overhang. To get past an overhang without slamming into the rock under it, slow as you go over the lip, and with your feet on the edge drop your buttocks as far as you can so that the rope is close to the rock face. That way when you drop over the edge, the rope won't swing you into the rock. Once you are descending while free hanging (meaning your feet aren't touching the wall), you will likely find yourself spinning slowly as twists in the rope unwind.

A friend of ours was practicing her rope skills prior to a race, and while waiting on the rope for her teammates to clear an overhang above her, she began to spin slowly on the rope. She reached out to grab the rock to stop her from spinning, and a piece of rock dislodged, falling and slicing through her hand. She required surgery to repair the tendons in her hand, and many months of therapy.

During the rappel the friction will create plenty of heat. It is advisable, and often mandatory, in races to wear protective gloves that have a leather palm to protect your hands.

To rappel with a heavy pack, attach the pack so that it hangs directly below you as you descend. This is recommended, and sometimes required, in races if the pack weighs a lot and could potentially pull you over backward so that you are hanging upside down on the rappel.

It is always good practice to include a safety backup system on the rappel so that if something happens and you do accidentally let go of the rope, your descent will be arrested until help can reach you. The typical system used in a race is either the "fireman" belay, or bottom belay, or the safety prusik.

In the bottom belay an individual is at the bottom of the rappel holding loosely onto the rope as the person descends. In the event of trouble, the bottom belayer simply pulls down on the rope. This provides sufficient additional friction to stop the person's descent.

A safety prusik loop is a short rope that is attached to the main descending rope with a friction prusik knot and then attached to the rappeler's harness. The prusik knot will easily slide over the main rope when the rappeller moves the prusik knot down the rope and no tension is placed on it. When tension is placed on the prusik knot (when the rappeller lets go of the prusik knot), it tightens around the main line and stops the descent. The easiest system to use is one in which the prusik is attached to the rope below the descending device and attached to the harness leg loop of the rappeler's harness. If the prusik catches, it can easily be released without requiring additional gear.

This prusik backup system below the rappel device uses the least and lightest equipment and is, therefore, a good one to know for adventure racing. It is widely used by professional mountain guides and search and rescue teams. The system is set up by attaching the rappel device to the climbing harness at the belay loop (normal position for the rappel), then attaching the prusik loop to the rope below the rappel device (where the brake hand will be on the main rope) as well as to the leg loop of the climbing harness using a locking carabiner (oval or D-shaped metal connectors used to link parts of a rope system). The prusik is then "minded" (moved down the rope) using the brake hand.

If something happens and the brake hand is released from the prusik, the prusik knot will catch on the main line and stop the descent. To begin descending again, the rappeller simply grasps the knot with the brake hand, loosens it, and begins to pull it down the main line again as he or she descends.

When the prusik is placed on the main line above the descending device, it becomes difficult to loosen the prusik knot once it catches on the main line without first unweighting the knot. This can be time-consuming and require the use of foot loops to stand on when you are doing a free hanging rappel. The most experienced team member should descend beside or behind a less experienced person in order to provide encouragement or assistance if needed. Once down, the first person can provide a bottom belay if the race staff is not providing it or if a safety has not been required.

When rappelling, watch for loose clothing, pack straps, long hair, or anything that could potentially get caught and pulled through the descending device. Always check each team member's gear before starting the rappel: Is the harness on properly? Is the descending device set up right? Are all carabiners locked? Usually there will be safety staff at the site to help out and make sure these things are done correctly; however, it never hurts for you to also check your team.

AN EASY SAFETY BACKUP FOR RAPPELS

Prusik loops placed below the rappel device can be made from a piece of 7 millimeter static cord 105 centimeters long and knotted into a loop using a double fisherman knot that leaves tails of 4 centimeters after the double fisherman knot is tightened. The completed prusik loop should be about 30 centimeters in diameter—short enough that it does not get jammed into the rappel device when released, and not so short that it is awkward and slow to descend. Try the system out and make sure the prusik loop is the right length for you.

ASCENDING ON FIXED ROPES

Another rope skill often utilized is an ascent up a fixed rope. There are many different techniques for doing this, so it is recommended that you obtain professional guidance and training, find a system that is comfortable and works well for you, and stick with it. Ascending can be against a less-than-vertical rock face or up a free-hanging fixed rope. Ascending is accomplished by using mechanical ascenders or friction prusik knots that grab the rope and will only slide up the rope.

A fixed rope ascent.
© 1996 Dan Campbell

ASCENDING SYSTEM SETUP

The equipment usually required for ascending in an adventure race consists of two mechanical ascenders, one or two foot loops, two daisy chains (attachment slings), three carabiners (two for the system, one for your harness), and a safety prusik (optional, for added safety). Mechanical ascenders utilize an offset camming action to grab the rope and prevent it from sliding down the rope. Many styles of ascenders exist; handled ascenders that have teeth to grab the rope include Clog, Petzl, and Jumar. To set up one type of ascending system:

1. Attach a single foot loop to your left-hand ascender using a carabiner.
2. Attach a daisy chain to your climbing harness using a simple girth hitch knot or clip one end of the daisy chain with a carabiner that is hooked to your harness.
3. Attach the other end of the daisy chain to the carabiner holding the foot loop on the left-hand ascender.
4. Attach a second daisy chain to your climbing harness using a girth hitch knot or carabiner.

5. Attach the second daisy chain to a carabiner attached to your right-hand (adjust the length so that when you push the ascender up the rope, you can't overextend your right arm—there should be a slight bend in your elbow).

6. Optional safety for three points of contact: Attach a safety prusik to the main line rope between the two ascenders and clip the end to the carabiner on your harness. The safety prusik needs to be long enough to attach from your climbing harness to the main line midway between the two mechanical ascenders (roughly 20 to 30 inches).

PLACEMENT ON THE MAIN LINE ROPE (FROM THE TOP DOWN)

Attach the right-hand ascender to the main line. Attach the left-hand ascender to the main line below the right-hand ascender. (Optional: Attach a safety prusik in between the two ascenders.)

ASCENDING TECHNIQUE

Use an inchworm technique to ascend on the rope. While standing in your left foot loop, push the right-hand ascender almost to arm's length (but not quite so it won't be out of reach!). Then sit in your harness and at the same time push the left-hand ascender up the rope while raising your left leg, almost to the right-hand ascender (leave a little space so they don't get hung up on each other). Next, stand up on your left leg and again push the right-hand ascender up the rope. Continue shifting your weight and moving up the rope in this manner, sit, stand, sit, stand, and so on.

Remember to keep the body vertical (into the rock) and advance the right- and left-hand ascenders alternately. The safety prusik will advance auto-matically as you ascend.

If you need to advance over a lip in the rock (usually at the end of the climb) and the rope and ascenders are jammed tight against the rock—bring your feet up and push out against the rock to pull the rope away from the rock. You can then advance the ascender up the rope. Other ascending systems use two foot loops and a technique that allows you to "walk" up the rope.

Regardless of which system you use for ascending, take the time to fine tune it to your height and build. A good system should make rope ascending

Spectacular Tyrolean traverse over a waterfall.
© 1999 Darrin Eisman

smooth and no harder than climbing a ladder. The system should make use of your legs, which are stronger than your arms.

THE TYROLEAN TRAVERSE

The Tyrolean traverse, also known as a flying fox, highline, or zip line, is another of the rope travel techniques you will encounter in adventure racing. These rope systems are designed to provide a way to traverse across a deep canyon or river from one side to the other. The competitor simply clips into the traverse line or pulley system (typically using carabiners) and slides along the rope using gravity to travel. Often the competitors must pull themselves across the last bit of the traverse because of the upward slope of the rope to the other anchor.

MOUNTAIN TRAVEL

Advanced mountaineering skills involve the use of ice axes, crampons, and other equipment. These skills require a high level of experience and can include glacier travel and travel over snow and ice, exposed rocks, and talus and scree slopes. Advanced mountaineering skills are usually only needed in long, expedition-style races.

Along with skis and snowshoes, ice axes and crampons are two essential pieces of equipment for basic snow travel. An ice ax is used primarily to provide balance and to stop a fall on snow. Crampons are designed to provide additional traction on snow or ice that is too hard and slick for comfortable travel in shoes or boots. Crampons can be rigid, which is the style typically used in ice climbing, or hinged, for general mountaineering typical of adventure races. Particularly useful in many adventure races are the partial, or instep crampons, which can provide the extra traction needed to cross short snowfields and are fairly small and lightweight. Rubber slip-on short spikes can be used with any type of shoe to provide a small amount of additional traction on hard-packed snow.

Staying warm and navigating in snow are two challenges in adventure racing. Practice your compass ability and get specific navigation training for snow. Learn to layer your clothing and determine what you need to stay warm while racing. This takes practice—best done before the race. The key is to wear the right amount of clothing and to travel at a speed that will allow you to stay warm without sweating—so that if you have to stop for any reason, you will not be wet and begin to chill. Consider carrying packets of hand or toe warmers in cold conditions. They are small and can provide just the heat you need to prevent frostbite or hypothermia.

Some races may require roped team travel across snowfields or glaciers. Descriptions of the proper techniques used in snow travel, roped travel, and crampon and ice ax use are provided in books such as *Mountaineering: The*

USEFUL ADVENTURE KNOTS TO KNOW

It is useful to know how to tie several types of knots. You never know when it might come in handy—for example, tying items into the boat, setting up a safety rope during the race. Knots you should know include simple overhand, girth hitch, figure 8, bowline, and prusik knots. These knots as well as many other useful knots for adventure racing are described, along with drawings, in Craig Luebben's *Knots for Climbers* (Falcon Press, 1995). Get a short piece of rope and practice until you can tie each of these knots automatically.

Racers descend from the summit of Mount Tronador.
© 1999 Dan Campbell

Freedom of the Hills, 6th edition (Don Graydon and Kurt Hanson, eds., The Mountaineers, 1997). If you plan on doing a race that includes these skills, it is recommended that you get adequate training beforehand.

COLD WEATHER LIGHTING

Batteries don't last as long when used in cold weather—be sure to carry extra ones during a cold race. Before you discard batteries you think are dead, warm them up—they might not really be dead. The Petzl Arctic is a cold weather headlamp that uses a battery pouch suspended around the neck so that the battery can be kept inside the shirt close to the body to provide warmth and extend the life of the battery.

AVOID FROZEN WATER

Water bottles will freeze, especially if carried on the outside of your pack. Keep them upside down: Water freezes at the top first (or what is now the bottom), so you will have water to drink. If you are using a hydration system, when you are finished drinking blow the remaining water in your bladder hose back into the bladder to keep it from freezing in the tube.

CANYONEERING

Canyoneering is a sport that is rapidly finding its way into many adventure races. (In European countries canyoneering is called canyoning.) Canyoneering is simply trekking in canyons and waterways, usually incorporating the use of ropes to rappel down waterfalls or steep canyon walls. The equipment and clothing often used in canyoneering includes wetsuits (if the water is cold), water shoes (sandals or specialized, sticky soled water shoes), and climbing gear (helmet, harness, and descending devices).

Canyoneering.
© 2000 Salomon N.A./Thomas Zuccareno

In canyoneering competitors will likely be rappelling down cliffs through waterfalls, jumping into deep pools, swimming and running along waterways, and running through canyons (which includes wading through shallow pools and stepping along slick rocks). Keeping your gear dry can be difficult. Line your backpack with garbage bags and place everything inside that you want to keep dry in Ziploc bags. Unless your backpack has holes on the bottom for draining (such as the Salomon adventure packs), it will fill with water and become heavy. One option is to use one of the backpack dry bags available on the market, designed specifically for travel through water.

Staying warm can be tricky while canyoneering. In many races you will have to trek to the site—and carrying a neoprene wetsuit might be bulky and heavy. An alternative would be to wear a thermal stretch suit like scuba divers wear (our favorite is the AeroSkins of California suit) or, if the weather is mild, Lycra tights and a thermal top. We have found that wearing protective clothing is useful because there is a tendency to bang against rocks when rappelling and running over wet slippery rocks.

Rope skills in mountaineering, canyoneering, and snow travel present what is often the most exciting part of the race for many adventure racers. The rope skills can be as simple as a traverse across something (one of our winter races finished with a traverse across the front of the ski lodge!) or as specialized as those required in snow travel. Learn the skills required for each race and practice them under different conditions. The Discovery Channel Adventure Race 2000 in New Zealand had competitors traveling over glaciers and on high mountain ridges during cold, snowy conditions. Even experienced teams, like Team Explorer from the United States, with Will Burkhart and Chris Burgess, both experienced and accomplished expedition-style adventure racers, occasionally found themselves in precarious and challenging situations where they were glad they had the navigation and mountaineering skills necessary to safely complete the race.

© 2000 Dan Campbell

© 1995 Dan Campbell

© 1996 Dan Campbell

© 1996 Dan Campbell

© 2000 Phil Mislinski

© 2000 Phil Mislinski

© 1999 Darrin Eisman

© 1999 Darrin Eisman

© 2000 Phil Mislinski

© 1997 Dan Campbell

© 2000 Dan Campbell

CHAPTER 9

NAVIGATION

© 2000 Dan Campbell

More team disagreements, arguments, and general team disintegration occur over issues related to navigation. The team's ability to recover after they discover that they went the wrong way will determine the success or failure of the team as a whole, but it is obviously better if this problem can be avoided altogether.

Many excellent books have been written on navigation, and courses on "staying found" through navigation skills are being taught everywhere by local backcountry organizations. This chapter provides introductory material on navigation as it relates to adventure racing, though the skill of navigation cannot be emphasized enough for its importance not only in racing, but also for other outdoor activities.

In adventure racing many of the best navigators are those racers who received training in the military, who compete in the sport of orienteering, or who learned navigation skills at a young age. These people had to start by learning the basics of navigation—and so can you! Then it's important to practice your navigation skills frequently, in different types of terrain and conditions, especially if you hope to one day be the lead navigator for your adventure racing team.

The first key to navigation is to know at all times exactly where you are on the map and in what direction you are headed. This requires good map and compass skills. If the team can keep their location pinpointed on the map at all times, it is possible to locate the next checkpoint and select a route to get there. As soon as a team can no longer identify where they are on the map, it becomes difficult to determine where you should go to get to the next checkpoint. Always keep the map properly oriented, and constantly glance from the map to the terrain and back again.

In an adventure race there is typically one lead navigator, and they are the only person who keeps the maps. Ideally a team has a lead navigator and at least one backup navigator who can take over when the lead navigator needs to rest. Ideally everyone on the team is proficient at navigating, with at least two experts. Having others on the team experienced in navigation is beneficial because they provide additional sets of eyes and ears for navigation.

The team can be issued many maps for the race—in longer races there may be more than thirty! A good team navigator understands that they are the only one with the maps, and must, therefore, share information as the team travels. The more open the communication between the navigator and the team, the smoother and more enjoyable the race will be. The navigator should let the team know what lies ahead on the map for the upcoming section. For example, "We will be crossing two mountain ranges, gaining and losing roughly 500 meters each time before we reach the next checkpoint." As the team is traveling, the navigator can point out certain features on the map when they are noted in the field. This does a lot to keep the team upbeat and confident. Problems usually arise when the team doesn't know where they are going and, in turn, lose their confidence in the navigator.

Navigating for a team in an adventure race is a huge task, the least of which is the potential for getting blamed if anything goes wrong. Almost nothing is worse than discovering you have gone the wrong way—it can add hours of hardship to an already exhausted team and take a huge mental toll on everyone—so take your time and make sure that you know where you are at all times.

The navigator should assign tasks to team members. For instance, the navigator can have one person keep watch for a particular land feature (such

ITEMS THE NAVIGATOR SHOULD TAKE TO THE RACE— THE TOOL BOX

Rulers

Markers (a variety of
  colored highlighters)

Pencils

Erasers

Grid interpolator

Map Seal (by AquaSeal) or other means of
  waterproofing maps

Scissors

as a school or creek on the right) and have another team member who has a good sense of pacing let the navigator know when the team has traveled a certain distance. Another can pay attention to the direction of travel and let the navigator know if the team changes directions radically from a particular bearing. Actively involving the whole team in navigation can relieve some of the lead navigator's responsibility and make the race more fun for everyone.

Too often the team members rely on the navigator to find the way and tune out what surrounds them. Each team member needs to be aware of his or her surroundings at all times. A team member's value increases dramatically with the simple ability to take notice of things. A lot of what each team member can do to help navigate during a race occurs without the help of a compass or map. Begin to pay close attention to rocks, creeks, and man-made features as you pass them. Keep track of all trail and road intersections, and if you do have a compass, note the team's general direction of travel and communicate to the navigator when it changes. Use all of your senses—the sound of a river, or waterfalls, or traffic on a road can provide important navigation clues.

A simple yet valuable thing to do is occasionally look over your shoulder as you travel and take note of how things look "in reverse." You never know when you may need to backtrack—and everything will look quite different when going in the opposite direction. Early on in a seven-day race several years ago, our team trekked over a mountain range to the other side. We had no idea that on the last day of the race we would be crossing back over the same mountain. All of us wished we had been paying closer attention.

One important tool of adventure racing navigation is the use of "handrails," or linear features, to help the team stay on track and minimize the chance of getting lost. Navigating from one checkpoint to another is easier if you can follow a handrail that runs more or less parallel to the direction in which you want to go. Examples of good handrails are trails and roads, railroads, rivers, fences, power lines, and any large feature that will remain visible for a while (such as a mountain range that remains on your left while traveling north).

Distinct, permanent features, either natural or man-made, can also be used as a "backstop," or "catching" feature, when navigating. Backstops can let the team know if they have gone too far or if they have reached a point where they need to begin looking for something. Backstops are a great tool to help prevent a team from making a mistake. Examples of good backstops are

TRUST YOUR TEAM PLAN

During the Eco-Challenge 2000, our team left a transition area to begin a hiking section of the race. It was the middle of the night. Our understanding of the race instructions was that we were to cross a footbridge and take the first trail to the left, running parallel along the river. At the bridge we met a team we knew returning to the transition area. They had been searching for the trail for more than two hours and asked if we knew where to go. We told them it was the trail just after the bridge. They said that they had tried that trail, but that it came to a dead end after about a mile. Unfortunately, we took their word for it, even though we had our own clear navigation plan, and joined them in searching elsewhere for the correct trail.

In the dark and confusion we searched for almost two hours before we finally gathered our wits, left the other team, and went back to the original trail we planned to take. About a mile along the trail it did appear to end, but further searching showed us that downed trees only blocked the trail, then it reappeared again a little farther on. It was, indeed, the correct trail, but we had allowed our judgment to be challenged by another team. As a result, we did not make a critical dark zone that evening, ending our chances of finishing in the top ten. Stick to your own navigation plan, unless you have a solid reason to do otherwise.

marked borders (country, national park boundary), rivers, and power lines. To use a backstop, identify one—perhaps a bridge crossing a river—just past something you are looking for, such as a small trail leading off to the left from the one you're on. If the team comes to the bridge without seeing the trail, you know you have probably gone too far and should backtrack to look more closely for evidence of the correct trail.

Another unique aspect of adventure racing is that if you are not the lead team, you can use the teams that have gone ahead of you to provide some information. This is not to say that your navigation plan should be to blindly follow all of the teams ahead of you—you might find that you are *all* lost. However, occasionally it is reassuring to make a decision and then note that many other teams have also passed the same way. Look for footprints that are fresh and bicycle tire tracks on dirt roads at intersections. We cannot emphasize enough, though, the danger in blindly following the tracks of other teams. It is always best to make your decision first and then take note of what other teams have done. If everyone seems to have gone the other way, it might be wise to at least take the time to re-examine the map and race instructions.

MAPS

Topographical maps are drawings that show the shape of the land surface. Contour, or elevation, lines are used to show where mountains, valleys, and canyons are, and provide a precise representation of the geography. Each contour line connects points of equal elevation. Every fifth contour line is an index contour line, which is darker in color than other contour lines and has the elevation written on it.

The contour interval, or distance between contour lines, can usually be found in the margin at the bottom of the map. This interval is very important and helps you to determine what terrain might be best to travel across. Closely spaced intervals on the map indicate areas that are steep and difficult to cross, while widely spaced intervals generally show an area that is relatively open and probably easier to travel through. Contours that form circles, with each one getting smaller, represent hills and mountains. When contours form a *V*, it is representative of a canyon or sloping ridge. If the narrow part of the *V* points upward to higher elevations, it indicates a canyon, or drainage; if the narrow end of the *V* points downhill to lower elevations, it indicates a ridge. *U* shapes are similar but indicate less steep canyons, and valleys that are more gentle and easier to travel through.

Maps provided in adventure races can be original topographic images or copies of the original maps. In most cases teams are given original color maps, though some races have been known to provide black and white copies of the original. Unfortunately, black and white maps lose some important detail. How useful the maps are will depend on who produced them and how long ago. The date the map was first produced is usually provided in the bottom margin. The date of any updates to the map will also be shown.

Color features of interest on a topographical map include the brown contour lines, green areas that depict forest or vegetation, blue indicating water (rivers, streams, lakes, oceans) and white showing open areas. Black is used to show man-made features such as buildings, roads, and trails. Other common features on maps include man-made buildings, such as schools, churches, and mines. Red is used to mark major roads and survey information. Occasionally purple is used to indicate a feature added since the original map was drawn.

The "scale" of a map refers to the size representation of the map. For example, a 1:24,000 map (a typical U.S. Geological Survey, or USGS, map) means that 1 inch is equal to 2,000 feet (1 unit of measurement = 24,000 units of the same measurement). The most common scale you are likely to encounter in a race outside of the United States is 1:25,000.

KEEPING YOUR MAP SAFE

Map cases are quite useful in an adventure race. They are designed to be worn around the neck and keep the map dry. Many people

choose to use a simple Ziploc bag to hold the maps for the race, yet having them readily available around your neck can be an advantage. If you are holding them in your hand, there is the potential to drop them. Our team once lost their map in the Southern Traverse race in New Zealand because of this.

Ian Adamson, lead navigator for Team Eco-Internet, uses a map case to keep his maps dry.
© 2000 Darrin Eisman

Commonly used topographical maps in the United States include USGS maps (often more than twenty years old) and privately printed maps, such as those from Trails Illustrated, DeLorme, and others. When racing in foreign countries, the maps you will be provided with are often military maps, whose detail can be very good, or very questionable. Always ask the race director what kind of maps you will be provided with and what the scale will be, so you can practice.

MAP COORDINATE SYSTEMS

The most common coordinate system encountered in an adventure race is the Universal Transverse Mercator, or UTM, system. Each map has a pattern of squares called grid coordinates printed on it. The UTM system is based on metric measurement and can be easily scaled down to the most convenient metric unit (kilometer, meter). Using the UTM coordinate system, every location on a map can be described by a unique set of map coordinates.

Maps are produced with markings along the border (blue tick marks on USGS maps, black marks on others) that represent 1,000-meter grids. The lines may or may not be drawn all the way across the map. If the lines are not drawn across the map, it might be useful to at least take the time to draw them in the areas of the map that you will be using (placement of your UTM coordinates on the map is important). In an adventure race you will typically be given one set of coordinates for each point. Plotting

WATERPROOFING YOUR MAPS

If you have time before the start of the race, it is a good idea to waterproof your maps. The maps may be exposed to rain, snow, and water during the race. Many people use laminating products, and several new products, such as MapSeal, that you can just brush or paint onto the maps, are now available. We used this product in the Raid Gauloises.

Plotting map coordinates on topographical maps.
© 1999 Darrin Eisman

a point accurately can put you within 100 meters of the actual location. Familiarize yourself with the UTM system and learn how to plot points. Everyone on the team can do this, and should. Don't forget to ask the race director how the checkpoint location information will be provided.

RACE NAVIGATION

What do you do with the map(s) once you get the race instructions and map coordinates? If you have multiple maps, it is crucial that you manage them carefully:

1.   Number each map and put the number on the race instructions in the area where the map is called out so it is easy to get the correct map out quickly.
2.   Mark all of the UTM coordinates on the maps (in pencil for the first time!).
3.   Have another knowledgeable teammate or support person double-check your UTM placement.
4.   Mark each UTM with a highlighter so it can be seen easily and name it (CP1, CP2, TA1).
5.   When all coordinates are marked, reread instructions and select a tentative route from one checkpoint to the next.
6.   Mark the tentative route with a highlighter.
7.   Make any notes from the race instructions that you need in the margins of the maps.
8.   Waterproof the maps, if possible.

It is always worthwhile to have someone check the UTM or coordinate placement to see if it is correct and makes sense. Race directors have been known to make mistakes, so if a point is counterintuitive (in other words, if the checkpoint on a trek is located in the middle of a lake), *ask*. Having several team members check the UTM plotting also gives everyone a chance to become familiar with the racecourse and begin to mentally prepare for it.

A USEFUL MAP TOOL

It is extremely handy to have a clear plastic grid called an interpolator to use to locate and mark the coordinates on the map. For example, for a 1:24,000 scale topographical map, a 10 × 10 grid where each line represents 100 meters is used that fits over one UTM square. This allows you to pinpoint the UTM location within 100 meters. Grids that will interpolate coordinates on a variety of scale maps are commercially available.

BE CAREFUL WHAT YOU CUT!

During one expedition-length race that included many maps, one of the favored teams plotted all of the coordinates and then trimmed off parts of the map that were outside of the defined race course, to reduce bulk and weight. Unfortunately, during the race they became lost, and were no longer on the part of the maps that they had saved.

Adventure races occasionally provide the chance to be creative when selecting a route to take. Remember, there are many ways to get from one point to the next. When selecting the tentative route the team plans to take, pay special attention to less obvious and less direct roads and rail lines that may be easier and faster to travel; or, conversely, look at more direct routes if the terrain is easy to travel across. Many factors go into selecting the route, and the route may need to be revised many times once in the field. For example, it the team origi- nally hoped to go off trail and take a direct route to the next checkpoint over some rough terrain, they many find that one of their teammates has severe blis- ters and thus decide that even though the regular trail is slightly longer, the foot- ing is better for their injured teammate.

If provided with the entire race course and all the maps at the start of the race, many teams wonder whether they should take the time to plot the whole course or just the first section, get going, and plan to plot the rest "on the fly." Although there are many considerations for most teams, the entire course should be plotted when everyone is fresh and rested. Trying to plot the course in the rain or when no one has slept in forty-eight hours can be difficult and poten- tially race-ending, if things are plotted incorrectly.

COMPASS

The compass you choose to use in an adventure race should be based on per- sonal preference and ease of use. Many racers use a compass with a sighting mirror, for more accurate triangulation and because it can be used as a signaling mirror in an emergency (mirrors are often mandatory gear, so a compass with

DECLINATION

Declination is the difference between magnetic north (the direction the magnetic needle points) and true north (the geographic spot map makers mark as the North Pole). Declination can be either east or west and is usually indicated with an arrow on the margin of the map. The declination arrow shows the correction that is necessary to account for magnetic variation. If the declination is 11 degrees east, it will be subtracted to correct your bearing. A common navigation saying to remember this is: "West is best [add] and east is least [subtract]." Declination adjustments can be crucial—without them you can quickly be off your target. Some compasses can be preset to adjust for declination, so you don't have to do the math when you are tired. Alternatively the map can be changed to account for magnetic declination. This is done by drawing parallel lines equal to the magnetic declination across the map. In this way both the map and the compass speak the same language— magnetic north.

one built in serves two functions). Another type of compass, often used by the international teams, is the basic orienteering sport compass that fits on the thumb so that when you are holding the map, the compass is always on the map. While the lead navigator will typically use a standard compass during the race, other team members often use an electronic compass that is built in to their watch (Sunnto, Casio, and others).

A standard compass is simply a magnetized strip of steel, balanced on a pinpoint and free to swing in any direction. Become familiar with your compass and how to use it, including understanding the proper names for the parts; how to hold it properly; how to adjust for declination; and how to use the compass to orient your map, take bearings, and to navigate.

ALTIMETERS

Another important tool that can assist in navigation is an altimeter. This instrument tells you the elevation you are at. It measures the barometric pressure and then converts it to the altitude at that location. Because the altimeter is so dependent on barometric pressure, which can change during a race, it is advisable to recalibrate the altimeter whenever you reach a known elevation point during the race.

Every team would be wise to carry and use at least one altimeter. Many adventure races require that competitors carry altimeters.

GLOBAL POSITIONING SYSTEM (GPS)

A global positioning system is an electronic navigation system developed for use by the military. The system uses satellites to pinpoint the location of the GPS unit and provides a coordinate for the location. GPSs are not currently allowed in adventure races, though there are some exceptions to this rule (notably the Raid Gauloises in 2000). Even when a GPS is allowed, each team still must be able to read the map and select the best route of travel. One of the most important uses of a GPS is that it can help the team locate where they are on the map if they have lost track of their position.

SOUTHERN HEMISPHERE COMPASSES

For adventure races held south of the equator, make sure you use a compass designed for Southern Hemisphere use. In the Southern Hemisphere, the curvature of the earth can cause the needle of a Northern Hemisphere compass to hit the bottom of the compass, rather than float free, and can result in erroneous readings.

ADVANCED SKILLS

Teams often encounter situations in races where navigation becomes very difficult, such as navigating at night, and when no landmarks are visible (fog, whiteout conditions, jungles, deserts). Night navigation is aided if there is a full moon. If you are racing in the Northern Hemisphere and it is a clear night, the North Star can be used for simple navigation. Because the North Star remains in one place, it is always located to the north of you. For everything else, it is recommended that you expand your skills by taking advanced navigation courses and practicing in all conditions at locations you are familiar with.

Finally, what should you do when, in spite of your navigating skill, you are in doubt about where you are? If something doesn't look right—if there is a feature on the map that you don't see around you—stop immediately and reorient yourself. Don't just keep going; things are likely to only get worse.

Instead, try to stay calm and think it through. Be sure the map is oriented correctly, and identify any obvious features or patterns. Have each team member go a short distance in different directions, returning to report what they have seen. Reconstruct your route from the last known position, then backtrack in the direction you came from until you start to see familiar features and reorient yourself to those.

Once you correct your mistake and are ready to continue, remember to study the map repeatedly to confirm where you are and then trust your compass to get you to your destination. Know the direction in which you are going, according to your compass, and know where you are on the map. The more you can practice your navigation skills, the less likely you are to become lost.

CHAPTER 10

OTHER DISCIPLINES

Use of exotic animals in adventure races.
© 1998 Dan Campbell

Many unique or less mainstream disciplines have been included in adventure races over the years. The Mild Seven Outdoor Quest in China and the Salomon X-Adventure series routinely include inline skating, both on-road and off-road, in their races. The expedition-style races often attempt to include events that are novel or that utilize equipment unique or indigenous to the area in which the race is taking place.

The Eco-Challenge 2000 included perahu outrigger sailing in boats made locally for the race. Scuba diving to an underwater checkpoint was also included for the first time, because the diving in Borneo is some of the best in the world. Originally, the Raid Gauloises 2000 announced that the trans-Himalayan race in Tibet would include paragliding. However, due to the unpredictable nature of the winds in the area, it was removed from the race. Another sport introduced in the Eco-Challenge 1998 in Morocco was "coasteering," an event similar to canyoneering, but which takes place along a coastline. When

Negotiating the slippery rocks while coasteering in Morocco.
© 1998 Dan Campbell

Perahu outrigger sailing at the Sea of China.
© 2000 Dan Campbell

coasteering, competitors are in and out of the water as they travel the coastline, especially when the race takes place along an ocean coast and the tides begin to change.

Competitors in the Eco-Challenge 1998 started the race riding camels. Since nearly all of the competitors had never been around camels, much less had the opportunity to ride them, they were given instruction and a chance to practice before the start of the race.

The introduction of these "new" sports into adventure races provides some of the overall appeal of competing—the opportunity to learn a new skill.

Inline skating in Aspen, Colorado.
© 2000 Salomon N.A./Thomas Zuccareno

We learned to inline skate just six weeks before competing in the Mild Seven Outdoor Quest 2000. While hesitant and tentative at first, we ended up loving the sport and will continue to incorporate it into our training routine. The introduction of new sports sometimes even forces the top adventure racers to learn something new. For example, every competitor in the Eco-Challenge 2000 needed to have both basic and advanced certification in scuba diving in order to be prepared to navigate underwater at night. Ian Adamson, of the winning Salomon Eco-Internet team, finished his last checkout dive just days before leaving for Borneo and the race.

Other unique events in adventure races have included sky diving at the start of the Raid Gauloises. As new sports become popular somewhere in the world, they will find their way into adventure races. Whitewater swimming, or hydro-speed, is a sport popular in Europe that was included in the Raid Gauloises 2000. Participants navigate moving rivers through whitewater using a type of float or boogie board. The Expedition Mata Atlantica 1999 also included whitewater swimming called Bahia-Cross in their country, and more adventure races will probably include some form of this sport in the years to come.

Another event beginning to show up in many races is the sport of caving, where competitors navigate their way through large caves, often with rivers running through them. Typically the caves are marked with glow sticks or string to

Hydro-speed at the
Raid Gauloises 2000.
© 2000 Pam Stevenson

PRE-RACE TRAINING AND TESTING

For the Raid Gauloises 2000 participants were required to attend a weekend of training in hydro-speed, rafting, canoeing, and rope skills prior to the race. Each participant was able to learn the required skills and practice with the equipment that was used in the race. Classes were held on the East Coast (New River in Virginia) and on the West Coast (American River in California). Participants had to travel to these locations and pay for the classes at their own expense.

follow so that the event becomes a speed issue, not a navigation issue. Because the safety of each team is paramount to race directors, precautions are taken to prevent teams from getting lost in a potentially dangerous location. Often caving is included in the race to showcase spectacular natural features of the area.

Caving was included in the Expedition Mata Atlantica 1999 in Brazil. Our team included two fairly big guys. They found themselves pushing their packs through small tight openings in the rock and then trying to contort their way through, often going feet first into the unknown. This was one place where the smaller women had the

FOR THE FUN OF IT

In the Expedition Mata Atlantica 1999, Team Brazil 500 completed the caving section and were told that they had gone through the cave with the second fastest time. When they heard this, they ran around to the cave entrance and went through a second time to see if they could beat the record . . . they did.

definite advantage—it was amazing to watch the big guys work their way through some of the narrow spaces.

Winter adventure races, or races that occur in locations with year-round snow, can include additional unique events, such as human-powered "dog-sledding," or polking, and ski-joring, where a horse or dog pulls teammates on skis, and sledding, skiing, and snowshoeing. Our Salomon Winter Adventure Race in the Rocky Mountains includes some unique events, including in 2000 a biathlon where teams cross-country skied and stopped to complete a Frisbee golf course at the same time.

Ride and run.
© 1995 Dan Campbell

Some form of team biathlon is consistently included in races such as the Mild Seven Outdoor Quest in China, Salomon X-Adventure races, Raid Aventura in Argentina, and many others. Team biathlon consists of a style of the Levi Ride and Tie format races, where teams are given one or two horses or bikes, and the competitors on a team can switch riders as often as they like.

Although learning new skills and sports provides one of the most appealing aspects of adventure racing, it can also place an additional financial burden on participants. The cost of obtaining our advanced scuba certification was between $500 and $1,000, for example, and had paragliding not been removed from the Raid Gauloises 2000, the cost for lessons just to become proficient in that sport would have been high.

CHAPTER 11

TRAINING FOR ADVENTURE RACING

© 1999 Darrin Eisman

By now the question you may be asking is: "How do I train to have a successful race?" Does "successful" mean finish? Or win? Or somewhere in between? John Howard, arguably the best expedition-length adventure racer in the world and identified as one of the top twenty-five athletes in 2000 by *Outside Magazine*, in a 1997 interview, said, "You don't have to be superfit, but you have to be sensible. If you take the position that you are just trying to get through it, you'll be all right. Of course, you do have to put forth some effort."

A lot of the top adventure racers consider adventure racing a lifestyle, meaning that even without the races, they would still be hiking, biking, paddling, and climbing mountains. Ian Adamson, who has won every major adventure race in the world, doesn't have a rigid training schedule—he just does what he loves. So what kind of training do you need? To be successful on all levels of adventure racing, you need a good endurance and strength base combined with the requisite skills and the right attitude. With the proper physical and mental preparation, you can greatly enhance your racing experience and level of success.

Many people entering the sport of adventure racing do so with a long, multiday race in mind, whereas others are interested in doing a shorter race. Identify the race you would like to do and then set some realistic goals.

Although the amount of time you will need for training will depend on your race goals, ten to twelve hours per week is enough to realize your potential for most races and still have time for other things.

We know competitors who entered the sport with a long race. However, because of the increasing availability of many good short races, we usually recommend that beginning racers start with one of those. A one-to-two-day race will provide the opportunity to race with a team; if longer than ten or twelve hours, it will give you the experience of racing at night. Most important, a short race will allow you to discover whether you even enjoy the sport, without a large investment of time and money. A risk of having a novice on a long race is that if they decide the sport isn't for them and quit midway through the race (and this has really happened!), they leave the rest of the team angry and frustrated, not to mention unranked.

COMPONENTS OF ADVENTURE RACING

There are four main components of adventure race training: (1) mental training, (2) endurance training, (3) strength training, and (4) skills training. Each component is important to the overall success of the individual and the team. In this section we will discuss these four components and give suggestions for optimizing your training. For specific training help, we suggest working with an expert in exercise and sports physiology. There are many good books written specifically for endurance training, such as *Serious Training for Endurance Athletes* (Rob Sleamaker and Ray Browning, Human Kinetics, 1996). (To see what some of the world's best adventure racers do to train, see Appendix B.)

MENTAL TRAINING

There is no question that success in adventure racing is a combination of mental toughness, focus, and desire, together with an ability to do the events and go the distance (endurance). In other words, success in adventure racing is not simply a physical matter. It is a matter of believing in your ability to do more than you think you can, having the right attitude to make it happen, and staying focused on the goal. With these things in mind, how can you train yourself to be mentally prepared for racing?

Confidence in your ability to "go the distance" is achieved by becoming comfortable with all of the skills that will be included in the race and doing the physical training necessary to build the stamina and strength you will need. Cultivate mental toughness by getting out and training when it is cold, rainy, and windy outside. Train both your mind and your body to endure a lack of comfort. Then, when faced with conditions in a race that make you cold, wet, and miserable, you will find yourself thinking, "I've been through this in training and I did it—and I can do it now." Overcoming challenges raises your level of confidence and your ability to persevere.

What you hold in your mind translates into your experience. Your attitude during training and racing determines your success or failure, so practice getting rid of the negative thoughts. In training, as soon as a negative thought creeps in (for example, "This hurts," "I'm tired," or "I'm cold"), replace it with a positive thought—change your mind. Look for the beauty around you, laugh with your teammates about where you are and what you are doing, and remind yourself how strong you really are. You will quickly begin to feel better and be reminded that you can do more than you think you can.

Focusing on your goal, both in training, and particularly during the race, will help you be in the right frame of mind when it counts. You need to want to be doing what you are doing each moment. Your mind can't be in one place while your body is struggling elsewhere! In training, practice using a mantra to stay focused. Team Salomon Eco-Internet used a mantra of "We will not finish second" to help win a hard-fought battle against Spie Battignoles in the Eco-Challenge 2000. Salomon Eco-Internet had finished second in the Salomon X-Adventure Race five weeks earlier—by forty-four seconds—and vowed not to let it happen again. It worked! Focusing, using mantras and meditation, are skills that you can and should practice in training.

What are the mental characteristics of the "successful" racer?

▲ The ability to be *flexible* in an ever-changing environment.

▲ A *positive* and *helpful* attitude.

▲ *Realistic* expectations of yourself, your teammates, and the race.

Cultivate these mental characteristics in your day-to-day life; they translate well to success in adventure racing.

ENDURANCE TRAINING

The greatest amount of your training will be spent in endurance training. If you are starting your training with little or no endurance foundation, the first thing you need to do is to build a reasonable base to train from. For most people this will take eight to twelve weeks of working on cardiovascular fitness. Take it slowly and focus on maintaining an aerobic heart rate. Endurance training involves building up to long workouts (more than one hour) at a fairly comfortable pace—on the bike, running, or whatever aerobic sport you enjoy.

Assuming that you already have a good endurance base, you need to continue to maintain it throughout the year. Endurance training is an important component of adventure racing because of the cardiovascular benefit, helping the heart more efficiently transport oxygen to the muscles and remove waste products (lactic acid) away from the muscles. Besides the many physiological benefits to endurance training, the sheer volume of it gets you ready to spend many long hours on your feet and on your seat. Endurance training is also the perfect opportunity to try out new things—new foods, hydration systems, and race clothing—and see what works for you.

The greatest amount of early endurance training should be done at 60 to 70 percent of the maximum heart rate in order to build the muscular endurance foundation necessary to allow the cardiovascular system and the lactate removal system to be stretched to the limit during interval and strength training. The book *Extreme Alpinism,* by Mark Twight and James Martin (The Mountaineers, 1999), provides a good description of advanced endurance training (they call it "cardiovascular power endurance") for alpinism. This training prepares you for high-effort bursts required for a fairly long period of time but from which you can still recover. In alpinism you can't rely on being able to run, hike, or climb a long distance slowly; occasionally you will find yourself in a situation (not unlike adventure racing) where it becomes critical to your safety or to beat a time cutoff to be able to move quickly through a tough section. For those of you who already have a strong endurance foundation, this training approach might be beneficial. It incorporates a combination of high-intensity endurance training with speed-strength intervals, recovery workouts, and lactate training.

An integral part of endurance training in the months prior to a race is the long, hard, back-to-back sports workout often called a "brick." This can include a hard paddle, immediately followed by a five-to-six-hour bike ride, and topped off with a run/hike. The idea is to use the entire body and imitate the stress of an adventure race as much as possible. Robyn Benincasa, of Team Salomon Eco-Internet, incorporates a hard brick workout (bike ride and run) into her training schedule once per week, beginning two months before a big race.

Following is a description, by discipline, of some of the things you can do during your endurance training. Use what we provide here as a guide, but tailor your own workouts to prepare you for the type of race you want to compete in. For each discipline we provide ideas for activities you can do indoors and outdoors, in the winter and summer. The actual amount of endurance training you do will depend on the length of the races you want to compete in. We did a significant amount of endurance training for the seven-to-ten-day Raid Gauloises and emphasized more strength/speed training for the four-day stage Mild Seven Outdoor Quest.

TREKKING

It is likely in the long races that you will encounter trekking sections that might take one or two days to complete. In two-day, weekend type races (twenty to forty hours), you might encounter a trekking section that covers 20 to 30 miles and takes four to eight hours to complete. How do you prepare your endurance for these long hours on your feet? By making long, slow trail runs and fast hikes with a pack as part of your standard training program. Regular trekking and running sessions of two to three hours, with occasional longer treks when time permits, have been enough to allow us to comfortably complete anything thrown our way in a race. One way to build a base for adventure racing is to train for an early season marathon. Remember that the greatest amount of your training will be endurance training—at a low intensity level, which trains your body to efficiently metabolize fat for the long haul.

Incorporate hills into your treks and runs as much as you can. You are not out for a hike with the family—push yourself a little. Trek hard up the hills and practice running down, but watch the knees (downhill running can be very hard on them). Train with a teammate, or find a training partner if possible, someone with similar goals who will motivate and push you a little.

In the winter you can usually continue to run and hike, and include other great aerobic sports such as snowshoeing and Nordic skiing to maintain and build your endurance base. Some of the best endurance athletes in the world are the elite Nordic skiers. If you find that you must go indoors during the winter, you can maintain your endurance base by training on equipment such as the treadmill, Nordic Track, elliptical trainer, and Stairmaster. For the Raid Gauloises 2000 we trained for many hours on the stair stepper while wearing heavy packs.

MOUNTAIN BIKING

The best way to build endurance for mountain biking is by road biking. Most of the world's top mountain bikers do a significant amount of their training on road bikes. The body tends to get beat up while mountain biking, due to the jarring and bumping on rough trails, so road riding allows the cyclist to train more often and longer. Can you do your road riding on a mountain bike? Absolutely, but a road bike is even better.

Find a group you can ride with so you can learn from the better riders and practice your "drafting" skills. Drafting involves forming a "pace line," where the team forms a single line, riding as close to the person in front of you as possible, gaining a drafting or airflow advantage, and making the whole team faster. Learn to look beyond the rear wheel you are following so that you will be prepared if something happens ahead of you. When taking the lead position, don't accelerate, or you will lose the whole team. Instead, maintain the same speed so you don't cause gaps. If you are leading a pace line and go uphill, don't stand up without giving a warning or else you are likely to bump the front wheel of the person behind you.

How often and how long should you ride? If you have the time available, try to incorporate at least two weekly road rides into your training schedule, of two to three hours, with a longer road ride of four to six hours every other week.

PADDLING

The same principal applies to endurance training as it does for paddling. In long adventure races you can be paddling nonstop for one to two days. Even in a twenty-four-hour race you could be doing a fairly long paddle of six to eight hours. How do you prepare for this? You need to try to incorporate long-distance paddles into your training on a fairly regular basis. This should consist of two to three hours whenever possible. This can be on lakes, or slow-moving rivers, or on the ocean.

If you are confined to the indoors, try rowing on an ergometer, or use a Nordic Track exercise machine, which, according to champion adventure racer and world-record endurance paddler Ian Adamson, is a great alternative to paddling because it works similar muscle group (plus the added bonus of the legs)!

Kayak training practice, a self-rescue technique.
© Darrin Eisman

CROSS-TRAINING

Currently some of the most successful adventure racers in the world come from a background of Nordic skiing. This fantastic sport provides tremendous endurance and strength training for both the upper and lower body. Another fun sport popular in Europe and growing in popularity in the United States is cyclo-cross, which incorporates road biking, mountain biking, running, climbing, and lifting your bike. Other options for cross-training are snowshoe running in the winter, and swimming year-round. All of these sports are great for building and maintaining endurance and will prevent your workouts from becoming monotonous.

STRENGTH TRAINING

What is strength training and what does it do? It typically involves lifting weights and doing strength intervals to increase the size and/or maximal strength of the muscles. Strength training will provide an increase in both strength and power, important for both the short and long adventure races. Strength is the ability to exert a given amount of force, and power is strength plus speed.

How does strength training enhance the endurance athlete's performance? Endurance performance is limited by weak links in the physiological system, so targeting any weak links with strength training can help our overall performance. For example, the paddler with a weak back will benefit their overall performance by strengthening the back using a weight program so that it no longer is the weak link in endurance. High-intensity training, or intervals, help to increase the maximal aerobic capacity, leading to increased endurance capability. In Norway and Finland, the top Nordic ski champions build their training around one or two hard interval sessions (four to eight minutes) to increase their aerobic capacity during the competitive season.

Weight training year-round will greatly increase both your strength and endurance for racing. We follow a weight routine provided to us by Scott Molina of triathlon fame, after he raced with us at the Mild Seven Outdoor Quest. Scott is a personal trainer and coach in New Zealand and quickly recognized that adding strength training to our training would help us overall in adventure racing. The program he devised includes strength training twice a week for the upper body and twice a week for the lower body.

SCOTT MOLINA'S WEIGHT WORKOUT FOR ADVENTURE RACERS

The best approach to strength training for endurance athletes is to spend three to four days per week in the gym with two days of upper-body emphasis and two days of lower-body emphasis. This schedule allows for important recovery time between workouts—the time when the body is getting stronger.

Each set of approximately twelve repetitions (reps) should take no longer than forty seconds including rest, and each total session should last only about thirty minutes. The program is set up to alternate between opposing muscles so you can go from one set to another with very little rest in between. For instance, bench presses and seated row work well together. Do a set of bench presses and then a set of seated rows and then go back to bench presses until you've done all of the sets for that pair, and then move on to the next pair.

In sets where the reps are decreasing, increase the weights. Select the weight so that on the heavy ones you feel at the end of the set like you could do no more than one more repetition.

Some of the exercises are a bit different than most people do them in the gym. On lunges take a big step forward, about 4 to 5 feet. The back leg stays very straight and the back foot is up on the toes. The feet don't move until you've done the required amount of reps, then you change legs and do the other leg. It is more of an up and down movement than a back-and-forth movement.

For the step onto a box exercise, touch the floor very lightly, making the leg that's up on the box do all of the work. Think of stepping down onto a carton of eggs without smashing them. For this exercise you alternate right and left legs, keeping one foot on the box at all times. The box should be about 1.5 feet high (pretty high).

Get help from a fitness instructor where you need to. It would be good to have a training partner who is stronger than you and really pushes you to the limit on these sessions. These workouts should be tough; they are not meant to be a nice, easy cruise along the trails!

Lower Body Day

Run or use stair stepper for twenty to thirty minutes to warm up.
Perform each set of two exercises alternately until completed.

Exercises	Sets	Repetitions
Swiss ball twisting crunches	3	16–25
Back extensions (hold a weight plate on chest)	3	10–20
Reverse crunches on steep incline board	2–3	10–20
Dumbbell (DB) dead lifts	2–3	10–20

Exercises (continued)	Sets	Repetitions
Leg press	3	15, 12, 8–10
Toe press (in the leg press)	3	15, 12, 8–10
Squats (deep, just below parallel)	2	15
Calf raises	2	15
Leg extensions (kind of fast)	3	15, 12, 8–10
Hamstring curls	2	12
DB lunges (hold DBs in hands)	2	15 (each leg)
Step onto box with DBs in hands	1	30–50 (alternate legs)

Upper Body Day

Swim or row twenty to thirty minutes to warm up.

Perform each set of two exercises alternately until completed.

Exercises	Sets	Repetitions
Hang from bar to stretch	2	20 seconds
Push-ups (ribs touch floor on each rep)	2	8–15
Bench press	3	15, 12, 8–10
Seated row	3	15, 12, 8–10
DB shoulder press	3	12
DB bicep curls	3	12
One-arm DB row (twist from waist, too) (Pull the DB to your hip. Think of pulling the cord to start a lawn mower.)	2	15 (each arm)
DB pullovers (big stretch, arms straight)	3	12
Triceps push-downs	3	12
DB shrugs (heavy!)	2	12
Wrist curls (both ways)	2	12
Trunk twist machine	3	15 (each way)

Along with weight training, work on strength for adventure racing by incorporating interval training. You can do intervals running, or fast hiking uphill, or biking to increase your trekking and mountain biking strength. One key to building strength on the bike is hills, hills, and more hills. Include hill repeats in all of your training. Team Nokia, winners of the Raid Gauloises in 2000, do some of their interval training by running or jumping up the stairs that take skiers to the top of the Nordic jumps.

Two tips for interval training:

1. Never do interval training unless you have the energy to do it properly; otherwise skip it or do it later in the week.

2. If you fall off the interval pace dramatically and can't maintain your speed without raising the heart rate, call it a day—don't overstress your system.

Strength gains obtained from lifting weights are quickly lost when lifting is ceased, so improve your strength year-round, not just in the months before a race.

SKILLS TRAINING

One of the most appealing aspects of adventure racing is learning new disciplines. Aside from the Kiwis, who seem to grow up kayaking, mountaineering, trail running, and orienteering, most of us must gain some new expertise in one or more of the activities typically found in an adventure race. Whether it is mountain biking or navigating, solo kayaking or rappelling, the more skilled you are, the more comfortable and confident you will be, thus making your entire experience a better one.

Skills training is done whenever you have a new discipline to learn, and when you want to sharpen or review your skills before a race. Another time for skills training is when the particular discipline in the upcoming race will be in terrain you are not used to. For example, before the Eco-Challenge 2000, some teams went to Florida, Hawaii, and Belize to practice jungle-type navigation and ocean paddling.

Following are some suggestions for skills training by discipline. Incorporate as many of these as you can into your training schedule.

TREKKING SKILLS

Trail running and trekking allow you to experience a variety of terrain, similar to what you are likely to encounter in a race. Run in mud, on the sides of hills, up creeks—whatever you can find that will give you the chance to practice your balance and increase your confidence for moving quickly over rough terrain and slick rocks. You will become more accustomed to staying light on your feet and making quick decisions to prevent slipping. In muddy conditions and on snow you will learn to look for rocks, roots, or anything else that you can step on to get better traction. Practice downhill running, letting gravity do the work. Being able to move quickly downhill is a combination of balance, being relaxed, quick thinking, and foot placement. Learn to trust your eyes and feet and look ahead down the trail. Strengthening your quadriceps will help your downhill running.

In an adventure race it is possible to be off-trail during a trek. Train by occasionally running or fast packing in the woods, off-trail. This will stress muscles and other body parts differently than trail running does; with practice, your ability to move quickly off-trail during a race will improve.

Trekking at night is fun and a great way to improve your night skills and confidence. Practice keeping your headlamp turned off, letting your eyes adjust to the dim light. We look forward to our nighttime workouts. We enjoy dinner with our spouses and children and then go hiking in the nearby mountains for several hours in the dark while the families are sleeping.

Go out when the conditions are less than ideal because this is a great way to improve your mental toughness and find out what clothing combinations work for you. Practice taking a shirt or jacket on and off without stopping and taking off your backpack. You will find that, with practice, you can do this easily by removing just one shoulder strap of your backpack, removing one sleeve, replacing the shoulder strap, and doing the same thing on the other side. Then stuff the shirt on the outside of your training partner's pack, or have them stuff it in yours. No stopping!

Become skilled at eating and drinking while you are trekking. Try different food combinations and make note of what works well for you. Compile a list of foods that you know you can eat and still trek or run without difficulty. Practice trekking with poles, and figure out how to best attach them to your backpack for easy "on and off" while you are walking. When trekking through thick brush or trees, poles in your hand and on your pack can become a nuisance, so learn how to pack them away so they won't catch on things and stop you in your tracks.

MOUNTAIN BIKING SKILLS

This is the time to get on the mountain bike and hit the trails, practicing balance and coordination. Focus on the skills you know you need to improve upon. Ride switchbacks and downhill, practice your bunny hop and other skills. Work on perfecting a smooth, round pedal stroke. Pull through the bottom of each stroke like you are scraping mud off of the bottom of your shoe. On the upstroke, pull the knee toward the handlebar. Learn to look up ahead on the trail—don't stare at what you want to avoid or you are guaranteed to hit it. One thing we like to do every spring is build a small skills course and spend time practicing on it.

MOUNTAIN BIKING SKILLS COURSE (SET UP IN A LARGE LOOP)

- ▲ Ride in and out of six water bottles spaced in a straight line 4 to 5 feet apart. (Tip: Look ahead, not down.)
- ▲ Stop completely and try to balance on the bike. (Tip: Level the pedals, turn the front wheel, and push lightly on the forward pedal to counter gravity.)
- ▲ Pedal across the length of an 8-to-10-foot narrow board.
- ▲ Practice high-speed cornering through three staggered water bottles, two staggered off to the right of the rider and one to the left. (Tip: Enter the corner just to the left of the first water bottle, steer just right of the second bottle, then exit the turn just left of the last bottle.)
- ▲ Do a timed wheelie; see how long you can stay up.
- ▲ Do a bunny hop over a small log.
- ▲ Carry your bike over a garbage can. Unclip right foot, swing over saddle and between the bike and your left leg. When right foot touches the ground, unclip left foot and begin to run, lifting the bike over the obstacle.
- ▲ Practice dexterity by slowing down, reaching over and picking up a water bottle off of the ground without stopping.

IT TAKES MORE THAN STRENGTH TO PADDLE

When it comes to overall speed and strength, Michael Tobin and Mike Vine are two of the best. They are elite cyclists and runners, finishing first and second in the 2000 XTERRA Off-Road Triathlon Series. They were invited to participate in the Mild Seven Outdoor Quest 2000, a multi-sport race with a significant amount of paddling. Our team, which included world-class triathletes Erin Baker and Scott Molina, was definitely on the weak side of the paddling scale. However, we had quite a laugh as we passed Tobin and Vine trying to maneuver their double kayak on the moving Yangtze River in China. It was vivid proof that strength cannot take the place of technique. It should be noted, however, that Team Bogner (Tobin and Vine's team) got the last laugh as they handily beat us in the overall race standings.

We have great fun setting up the course and doing timed loops through it, trying to get better on each loop. Other skills training ideas include doing a slow race where the last person to cross the finish line is the winner. It's great for balance and slow-speed bike handling.

Practice riding close to your training partner(s). Put an arm around one of them and pedal together. Being comfortable riding near other riders is important in an adventure race, especially when one team member is being towed or pushed. Practice towing your teammates and being towed under varying road/trail conditions. Learn to ride your bike with no hands—it will help your balance so that you are more comfortable when helping a teammate or when eating or changing gloves or your top while riding.

PADDLING SKILLS

First and foremost, if you don't know how to swim, learn. You must be able to swim to participate in adventure races that have paddling as a discipline.

The best way to improve your paddling skills is to get professional instruction. If you can't do that, try to find a local canoeing/kayaking club and start paddling with them. There will probably be some paddlers who are better than you who will be happy to give you pointers. Look into taking a raft guide course. Even if you do not plan to be a raft guide, some companies open their classes to the public. For example, Timeberline Tours, a company run by Billy Mattison (of Team Vail), holds a raft guide class every spring on the Colorado, Eagle, and Arkansas Rivers in Colorado. The class is open to people wanting to improve their river skills, if space is available. It is a great way to learn to read moving water and maneuver a boat, and become proficient in swift water rescue.

Rent boats you are not familiar with and try them out. If you only know how to kayak, find a canoe and learn to paddle it. If you are always in the front of a two-person kayak, climb in the back and learn how to make corrections to keep the boat on course. Try a boat with and without a rudder. If you only paddle on a lake, get on a river with an experienced person, or try sea kayaking.

Many pools have times set aside for kayak skills practice with experienced people on hand to help. It's a good opportunity to learn or practice the "Eskimo roll," a technique used to right a flipped kayak. If you have never been in a kayak with a spray skirt, learn to put it on without any help.

NAVIGATION SKILLS

Navigation does not require endurance and strength by itself. Practicing for navigation cannot be overemphasized. You need to be comfortable with the basic use of a map and compass, terrain association, and route finding. The best way to learn is to get out there and do it a lot, and under different conditions. Learn to read your map while on the move so that you don't have to stop frequently to look at it. This particular skill is harder to learn than it sounds. In Scandinavia, children learning orienteering are sent out on training runs with comic books to learn to read while they run. Try taking a section of the newspaper out with you on your next morning run!

Get instruction if you need it. Check at the local sporting goods shops and contact the local search and rescue group to find classes and field sessions on basic navigation. Find a local orienteering group and start participating in the meets. Orienteering meets are a great way to get practice in navigation. A Rogaine (rugged outdoor group activity involving navigation and endurance) is an event that takes up to twenty-four hours to complete—perfect training for the adventure racer.

Practice your visual distance estimation. As you become better at navigation you will naturally start to get used to what a pine tree looks like when it is 500 feet away or 200 feet away. One way to practice this skill for short distances is to place a flag on a tree, measure off a distance in an open field, study the tree from all angles at that distance, and then do the same thing at a farther distance. You can also practice this when you are hiking a known trail to a point with a known distance. For example, in Fort Collins, Colorado, we often run a trail to the top of Horsetooth Rock, a distance of about 5 miles. Horsetooth Rock and the surrounding trees are clearly visible throughout the entire run, affording the perfect opportunity to observe the change in the appearance of the trees the closer we get. Use your observation to become more confident of estimating distance.

Another way to estimate distance is by time. Establish what your team's pace is when traveling on different types of terrain. Locate a 2-to-3-mile course on (1) level ground such as a dirt road; (2) a moderately steep uphill trail; (3) a steep uphill climb on trail; and (4) all of the above, but off-trail. Time how long it takes you to walk 2 to 3 miles and determine your average walking pace for each of the different terrains. This can come in handy during a race to estimate the distance you have traveled.

Go with a training partner to an area you are familiar with when it is snowy or foggy and practice your navigation skills. Learn how to use a global positioning system; you never know when they will be allowed in races (they were permitted in the Raid Gauloises 2000 in Tibet.

MOUNTAINEERING AND ROPE SKILLS

Learning rope skills such as rappelling (descending), ascending, and traversing is necessary when those activities are present in a race. Most of the shorter adventure races will have a rappel and/or a Tyrolean traverse, while the longer races often include ascending in addition to the others. It is critical to have the basic knowledge and comfort level to perform these skills quickly and safely.

Learn the necessary skills by contacting climbing groups, climbing gyms, local mountaineering shops, and clubs that teach classes in rope techniques and/or mountaineering skills. Check among your friends and acquaintances to see if someone is knowledgeable and experienced in rappelling, ascending, snow or glacier travel, and self-rescue and whether you can tag along the next time they are going out to practice.

UNIQUE DISCIPLINES

Sometimes you will be required to learn specific skills just for the race you have chosen to do. As noted earlier, we had to learn to scuba dive and inline skate for races in 2000. We got our inline skates just six weeks before the race and immediately got an experienced inline skate instructor from the gym we work out at to teach us to skate. Our first lesson was confined to an outdoor basketball court at the local university—good thing, since we were pretty unsteady. He was able to teach us the basics and get us on our way. Now we both love the sport! Other sports you may need skills training in include horseback riding and sailing.

ALTITUDE TRAINING

Many adventure races, both in the United States and around the world, take place, at least partially, at high altitudes. Acclimatizing, or adapting to high altitude, before the race can be very helpful for those competitors who do not live and train at altitude. Salomon Eco-Internet spent one week training in and around Boulder, Colorado, getting ready for the Raid Gauloises 1999 in Ecuador. In 2000, the team (now Salomon Land Rover) spent the weeks before the Raid Gauloises training in Estes Park, Colorado, at 7,200 feet and higher before leaving for Tibet and Nepal. Our one teammate who did not live in Colorado came out to spend a week training in Leadville, Colorado, at 11,000 feet before leaving for the Raid. Partly due to this effort, perhaps, neither team had significant problems with altitude (over 17,000 feet) during the Raid, while many other teams did.

TAKING TIME OFF FROM TRAINING

A rest day can be a great time for incorporating some skills training, such as practicing your ascending and rappelling techniques, or having a day to reconnect with your family and literally do nothing. Some adventure racers routinely take one day off every week, others never take a day off from some form of training; after all, adventure racing is a lifestyle, so almost everything that we love to do counts as training.

What about tapering before a race? Resting before the race is definitely wise, just as it is in almost every sport. Most athletes use the tapering phase to continue to run or cycle easily to maintain circulation and raise the heart rate slightly. Tapering strategies vary depending on the race. In general, reduce the amount and intensity of your training in the weeks (for a long race) or days (for a short race) immediately prior to the event.

TREATISE ON TAPERING

Participation in the long races in foreign countries has its own forced tapering built in. Robert Nagle of Team Saloman Eco-Internet and one of the world's top adventure racers summed it up when he said the taper schedule consists of a week of crazed packing including:

▲ Last-minute calls to obtain obscure pieces of manda-tory gear.

▲ Saying goodbye to your spouse and explaining to your kids why you'll be away for a month.

▲ Paying gazillions of bills.

▲ Realizing your passport will expire while you are away and getting it renewed.

▲ Doing double time at your job to get everything you committed to completed.

▲ Getting last-minute shots (inoculations, that is, though you crave the other kind).

That last frantic week is followed by:

▲ Two days of sitting in airports.

▲ Desperate repacking at the ticket desk to meet weight restrictions.

▲ Grousing about all of the excess baggage payments.

▲ Discovering that half of your baggage didn't arrive with you.

▲ Nervously watching the gangs of teenagers with AK47s who are patrolling the airport.

- ▲ Sleeping on the airport tarmac atop your bags while waiting for someone to collect you.
- ▲ Returning to the airport for your missing baggage.
- ▲ Returning to the airport for the one or two of your teammates who missed their connections.
- ▲ Wanting to eat the local food but being a conscientious team player and abstaining so you won't get ill.
- ▲ Sneaking a fried banana at the local market.
- ▲ Visiting the porcelain throne (again and again and again . . .).
- ▲ Catching up with all those amazing people you haven't seen in a year.
- ▲ Trying to build a packing case.
- ▲ Trying to avoid the press (or desperately seeking them out, depending).

And finally, a chance to sleep during the opening ceremonies and race briefing and then:

- ▲ We gotta do the maps now???
- ▲ More crazed packing.
- ▲ Six hours or more so crunched over the maps you can't stand up straight.
- ▲ A sixteen-hour bus drive down dusty roads in 125-degree heat.
- ▲ Clamoring for the bus to stop (damn that fried banana).
- ▲ Crawling into a bivy bag in the pouring rain to sleep for ninety minutes before the start of the race.

TRAINING AS A TEAM

Wow . . . what a concept! Our strategy in putting our team together specifically for each race has typically not allowed us to train together as a team. However, if and whenever possible, this is clearly a huge benefit. The teamwork aspect of adventure racing is so paramount as it relates to a team's success that getting to know each other's strengths and weaknesses, likes and dislikes, how each one reacts to different situations, can only benefit a team at race time.

If you do not have the benefit of being able to train together much or at all prior to a race, e-mails and phone conversations help toward better understanding and bonding of the team. E-mails can give a good insight into individuals, and this is also used effectively to delegate who brings what mandatory gear to the race, as well as food and other supplies. All of this is part of the pre-race training, or team bonding process.

In summary, adventure racing, more than most other sports, combines a very high level of mental toughness with physical strength and endurance. You cannot be successful in adventure racing if you are lacking any of the necessary training components. There are no "cookbook recipes" or formal training programs (yet) in adventure racing. Many competitors feel that this is one of the appealing aspects of adventure racing and are disappointed to see the increase in competitors coming into the sport who want specific training programs and formulas similar to the regimented approach typical of triathlon training.

Contrary to popular belief, adventure racing and training is not a full-time job for most people. Success can be gained through a regular and steady regimen of skills development, endurance-oriented sessions, and strength workouts. Above all, have fun with your training. That's what adventure racing is all about.

"SYNERGY" IN TRAINING

Team Synergy, while training for the Eco-Challenge 1998 in Morocco, had each team member take a turn designing a multi-sport training day or small racecourse for every other or every third weekend of the month. The training was like doing a short course adventure race for eighteen to thirty hours. Having a different member set the course each time kept it fun, and it enhanced their team's synergy while providing excellent training weekends.

PART THREE

THE
RACE

CHAPTER 12

INTO THE NIGHT: ASPECTS OF NIGHT RACING

© 1995 Dan Campbell

One of the truly unique aspects of adventure racing is the experience of competing through the night. Whether it's trekking, mountain biking, paddling, or rappelling a 300-foot cliff, everything changes when the sun sets. Navigation becomes difficult, the pace gets slower, and the "sleep monster" begins to hit.

Some races institute "dark zones" when a section is considered too dangerous for completion in the dark. One example would be Class IV whitewater rafting, or canoeing Class III waters. In the Raid Gauloises 2000, for example, teams were ordered to pull off the water wherever they were at dusk. They were not allowed to continue until 5:30 a.m. when the sun began to rise—it was just too dangerous. A similar type of dark zone was imposed on one section of a river in the Eco-Challenge 2000; however, if teams made it past the most dangerous whitewater on the river before dark, they were allowed to continue because the river began to flatten out at that point.

Traveling at night is also quite a bit slower than daytime travel. When you are biking or trekking, plan on taking 20 to 30 percent more time to complete a section than you would during the day. Not only is biking or trekking more difficult, but paying attention to your route and navigation is much more challenging at night. This becomes important when you are estimating your travel time for a certain section of the race. If you are going to be traveling at night, be sure to add at least 25 percent to your normally anticipated travel time and plan accordingly. Failure to do this may result in running short or out of food and water, as well as not giving your support crew a good estimate of your arrival time.

Essential lighting for night travel (and part of any mandatory gear list) includes a headlamp and front and rear lighting for your bike.

HEADLAMPS

Using a headlamp at night is something you should practice before your first race. Train your eyes to become more accustomed and better at sight in the early moments of darkness. Learn to wait as long as possible before turning on your headlamp. There is a tendency for many beginning racers to turn on their light as soon as it becomes slightly dark. Yet it is oftentimes unnecessary and, as such, is a waste of valuable battery time. Another advantage to getting used to traveling without as much light comes into play when racing with a team. It is not necessary for everyone to always have their headlamp on; perhaps you can use one or two headlamps and keep the others turned off, which can dramatically conserve battery time.

Headlamps come in many sizes, with varying features. As with everything else, it is best to try different models and see which headlamp works best for you. Headlamp and bike light differences will include the number of batteries required (two versus four AAs, for example), weight, burn time (how long the batteries will last), and light output.

First, lets discuss the types of headlamps that are available. Most headlamps don't weigh very much—the weight penalty is in the batteries that are required and the need to carry replacement batteries for multiple nights' usage in expedition-length races. Two popular and inexpensive general-purpose headlights, the Princeton Tec Solo and the Petzl Micro, each use two AA batteries and weigh between 3 and 5 ounces without the batteries. Almost all headlamps can be used with either a standard krypton bulb or a halogen bulb, depending on your light output needs. The halogen bulb produces a very bright light, but burn times are much shorter than for a standard bulb. For example, both the Solo and the Micro will last for seven to nine hours using a standard bulb but only one to two hours using a halogen bulb.

Many adventure racers use headlamps that provide slightly more light, such as the Princeton Tec Vor Tec or the Petzl Zoom. The Vor Tec provides more light than the Solo (roughly double) but uses four AA batteries, which increases the weight to 8 ounces with batteries—all of it sitting on your forehead. The Petzl Zoom is designed to use with a flat 4.5-volt battery that sits on the back of the head, providing a balancing effect. The 4.5-volt batteries last roughly seventeen hours, or for two nights of racing.

Most headlamps have only one bulb in place at a time, but you can physically trade out a standard bulb for a halogen bulb. The downside is carrying an extra bulb and taking the time to change it when you may only need to use the halogen for a short period of time. One of the more popular adventure racing headlamps, the Petzl Duo, actually has both a halogen and a standard bulb that you can alternate between with the flick of a switch. The standard bulb will burn for eight to ten hours and the halogen bulb is good for two to three hours. The Duo weighs around 7 ounces, so while the versatility of the headlamp may be attractive, there can be a trade-off in weight.

Another style of headlamp that is sometimes used in adventure racing is the LED light, which is not as brilliant as the standard or halogen lights, but lasts a very long time. LED headlamps are compact and lightweight and have burn times of from 40 to more than 150 hours. The light output is diffuse, making the headlamps perfect for map reading and general trail use. Two examples are the Petzl Tikka, which weighs just 2.5 ounces with batteries (three AAAs), and the Princeton Tec Matrix, just 4.5 ounces with batteries (two AAs).

With all headlamps it is important to test your system and know how long you can expect the batteries to last. Lithium batteries are more expensive but can extend the burn time significantly. In cold weather the battery life is greatly reduced, so keep this in mind and plan accordingly. It is a good idea to carry extra batteries during a race so that you won't have to race without light. This is a consideration in the type of headlamp you choose—you probably don't want to be carrying three C cell batteries in your backpack.

Headlamps can often be worn either over or under a helmet (depending on the battery placement) for caving, rope skills, or biking. Try your headlamp on your helmet before the race and make sure it will work easily and is comfortable. Some racers attach clips to their helmet to hold the headlamp in place; others use Velcro. Having your headlamp pop off of your helmet (if on top) or fall down into your eyes (if underneath) can be both annoying and frustrating, so test out your system.

One phenomenon you might notice at night with a headlamp turned on is a sort of tunnel vision. The light cast by your headlamp seemingly creates a tunnel effect. Getting a light lower to the ground can help to provide greater distinction in the terrain, by casting more shadows; for this reason some competitors will occasionally carry their headlamps in their hand as they trek, which will also minimize the tunnel effect and provide a change of pace.

Out of courtesy, turn your headlamp off, or look away at an angle, when talking with a teammate or volunteer with your headlamp on. It is easy to spot the headlamps of other teams during the night, so consider traveling without lights, or with only one, when another team is trailing you or after you have just navigated a difficult section. This way you reduce the chance of another team keying off your path of travel or of possibly motivating them to catch your team. Conversely, if your team is less competitively motivated, there are times when you may want to use your lights to assist a trailing team in finding their way.

What happens when someone on your team has no light and no replacement batteries? Put someone with a light in front of that person, as well as someone behind them, if possible. Many people find that following someone who has a light is fairly easy, because you can step where they step or ride where they ride. This is a good skill to practice when you are out at night, for sooner or later it is bound to happen to you.

WHO TURNED OUT THE LIGHTS?

During a nighttime bike section of one of our MountainQuest races, one team had all of their headlamps and bike lights burn out. Safety personnel spotted the team and provided them with lights to get to the finish line. The team was assessed a time penalty for not having lights, but they arrived safely.

LIGHTING FOR
YOUR BIKE

Lighting systems are also necessary for night travel on your bike. A flashing red light on the rear of your bike (or you) is always required. There are many configurations and lighting systems used for biking in adventure races. When considering what system to use, consider the power output, burn time, weight, and expense. Probably even more consideration should be given to bike lighting/power output than with your headlamp.

Inexpensive lights ($10 to $20) actually may have a good burn time but will typically produce only 2.5 watts of power. There is a huge difference between this and, say, 5 or 10 watts of light output. Some riders set up two lights on the front of their bikes, or ride with both a light attached to the front of the bike and their headlamp as backup. For example, using a halogen Cateye light on the bike combined with a headlamp can provide sufficient light for most riding. If a section of the bike ride becomes fairly technical, both lights can be used at once, when the riding is easy and less light is required the halogen Cateye can be turned off to conserve the batteries.

High-tech lighting systems with a really bright output are available for bikes but can cost more than $200. Most of them use rechargeable batteries that have very short burn times, primarily designed for commuting in traffic. NiteRider makes an inexpensive light with a high 10-watt output that takes five D cell batteries in a battery holder that fits into a water bottle cage. The light will burn for six to eight hours—enough to get through one night of adventure racing. It is common for riders to use their headlamps as backup when night riding, particularly when looking for a trail off to the side, or other landmarks. You will be able to ride faster and with more confidence with a strong lighting system on your bike.

SLEEP AND
SLEEP DEPRIVATION

When we aren't racing we normally sleep eight to ten hours a night . . . and nap on occasion; in other words, we love our sleep. However, when we're in an expedition-length race, we will typically go about forty hours before we begin to feel the desperate need for some shut-eye. Generally your adrenaline and motivation will keep you going on the first night of the race. By the second night you may become tired, but it is probably much more mental than physical, and you have the help and support of your teammates to get through.

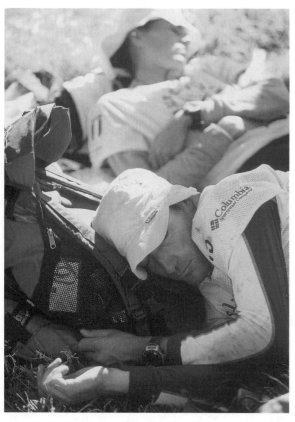

Catching some "Zs" in Australia.
© 1997 Dan Campbell

In a twenty-four-hour race it is not likely that your team will take the time to sleep, especially if your goal is to be competitive. If the race is longer, however, the lack of sleep can quickly begin to take a toll. Many experienced competitors feel that in the long expedition races it does not pay to become sleep deficient, because the potential for making mistakes, such as navigational errors, rapidly increases. Teams may decide to take a short rest as early as the second night of the race. The navigator on the team will probably need to sleep before the rest of the team, because they need to be mentally alert at all times, while the others can zone out.

Deciding where and when to sleep is an important team decision. There are many factors, including night-time versus daytime, how everyone feels, transition areas or shelters, cutoff times or dark zones, and weather.

Most of us are used to sleeping at night, when it is dark, so this is often when we are most likely to feel sleepy. Because the team is probably traveling slower at night, it can make sense to use some of this time to sleep, and plan to move faster during the daylight hours. A good time to sleep is just prior to sunrise, so you awake at daylight. Every day's sunrise seems to breathe new energy into your body.

If one person on a team is ultra-tired and wants to sleep but the rest of the team is feeling fine, the other teammates should do all they can to keep moving forward and help the tired person along. Talk with the person; sing with the person; do whatever is necessary. The only caveat here is if you are, per-haps, on a technical bike leg, it might be smarter to walk that section rather than risk serious injury. If most of the team is suffering from sleep deprivation and it is a cause for concern of injury, getting lost, or increased tension among team members, it is probably a good time to rest.

We tend to do a lot of singing when someone on the team gets tired. Singing medleys of oldies but goodies is our favorite way of keeping awake dur-ing the night hours. This tends to not only be fun and cause laughter but also forces you to use your mind in remembering the words and the songs. Other times, an "awake" team member may stay close to the tired person and force a conversation by asking questions about the other person's family, occupation, or philosophy. In spite of everyone's best intentions, sooner or later during an expedition-length race everyone will get sleepy. In Borneo, during the Eco-Challenge, while paddling in the perahu outrigger canoes just before sunrise, everyone became very tired. We agreed that two people would sleep while two people tried to stay awake and paddle. It didn't work, and soon all four of us were sound asleep and drifting in the Sea of China. Fortunately, Team Vail came upon us and after yelling at us for several minutes as they approached, we woke up and managed to keep from drifting off-course.

There are different philosophies on sleeping in transition areas. Some competitors prefer to sleep in a TA because there may be shelter, dry clothing, or other comforts. Conversely, some avoid sleeping in TAs for those very same rea-sons, rationalizing that you will waste more time there due to the conveniences. The teams of John Howard, one of the world's top adventure racers, have been known to come into a TA, see another team preparing to sleep, and quickly gather their gear and leave. What the other team doesn't know is that once

CREATIVE SHELTER

In the Eco-Challenge 2000, due to paddling restrictions in the dark, our Team Friction Free, was forced to pull over for the night. We were wet, cold, and it was raining. We strategically hoisted the canoe over a log on one end and a large rock on the other and were able to use it as a shelter from the storm.

away from the TA, Howard's team will probably stop to sleep, so the other team is left thinking that Howard's team is feeling stronger and gaining a big advantage on them.

An important factor to consider on length and timing of your sleep is where you are in the race relative to dark zones, race cut-offs, places where there may be a backup (ropes, for example), and TAs. If the team feels that they have a chance to make it through a dark zone or beat a race cut-off, stopping to sleep might not be advisable.

Weather is a consideration in choosing when and where to sleep. If it is raining or snowing and you come upon a shelter that you can use, it might be a good time to get some sleep. Most often, however, you will be sleeping outside, on the ground, and must make the best of a difficult situation. Some of the things that you can do to be more comfortable include using a foam pad as a ground pad (some backpacks have a removable foam pad in the back), an extra piece of clothing or your pack as a pillow, a garbage bag as a sleeping bag to provide partial cover or an emergency or space blanket to provide cover.

The best technique for creating warmth is by sleeping in a "puppy pile" with your teammates. Sleep front to back ("spooning") as a team, with the lucky (or coldest) ones in the center of the pile. In the rain, it is not uncommon for teams to huddle together under trees or rocks, sitting up and dozing.

We were, perhaps, one of the few teams to sleep in the jungle during the Eco-Challenge 2000. The jungle is not a pleasant place to take a nap, but we were able to use the lightweight hammocks we had to keep us off of the ground (and away from the leeches).

Emergency blankets are often required gear for an adventure race, and racers frequently use them for cover when sleeping. The downside to using an emergency blanket is that it is difficult to repack—you can rarely return one to its original volume.

Most competitive teams seldom sleep for more than two hours at a stretch. However, in the expedition-length races, there are often forced opportunities to sleep for longer periods of time. On the second day of the Raid Gauloises 2000, teams could not pass through the border from Tibet to Nepal after 3:30 p.m.—and the border didn't reopen until 8:00 a.m. the next morning. No teams made it through this dark zone and, in fact, Team Salomon Land Rover (Eco-Internet) was able to spend the night in a local hotel, eat dinner, sleep, and shower before the 8:00 a.m. border opening. Dark zones on river sections in the Raid Gauloises 2000 also provided almost every team with a chance to sleep for more than eight hours in the middle of the race.

One popular method of dealing with sleep deprivation is via "power naps" of fifteen to thirty minutes. These short naps can regenerate and refresh your mind and body sufficiently to get you going again.

Sleep deprivation affects one's coordination, judgment, mood, and propensity for injury. It is important for each team member to be aware of the others' status at all times. If someone is dozing off or literally walking in their sleep, take extra steps to keep the person awake. Some competitors resort to using some form of caffeine, such as a gel or chocolate coffee beans, when they begin to tire. Some adventure racers feel that popping caffeine pills or other over the counter stimulants to stay awake is counter to the spirit of adventure racing—not to mention that they could be bad for you—so consider your options carefully. In addition, beginning with the Eco-Challenge 2000, some races may institute random drug testing.

Hallucinations are a possible side effect of sleep deprivation. When your teammate starts talking about the monkey on your shoulder, for example (true

CAUSE FOR ALARM

For all rest breaks, but power naps especially, have a good alarm (usually one's watch) set. Every team can relate stories of oversleeping and not hearing their alarm. Be sure to have a solid sounding alarm and place it near your ear. Nothing is worse than losing an hour in a race due to negligent oversleeping. In the Raid Gauloises in Tibet and Nepal, our team stopped to catch a few hours of sleep before sunrise. Because it was cold, we all wore hats and were huddled down under our emergency blankets. Unfortunately, we ended up sleeping through four alarms and losing an hour of travel time.

situation), it's a good indication that they are hallucinating. Most people, however, seem to recognize the oddity of their visions and keep them to themselves. If you become aware of a teammate hallucinating, pay close attention for a bit, ensuring that the person stays with you and doesn't wander off or walk toward what they think they see. In most cases, sharing one's hallucination is cause for some good laughs and stories.

One of the most unique, challenging, and interesting aspects of adventure racing is traveling through the night. Being comfortable with night travel, wearing an extra layer or two of clothing for warmth, having teammates to support you, and being smart about resting will go a long way toward ensuring a successful racing experience.

CHAPTER 13

FUEL FOR RACING

© 2000 Liz Caldwell

There are as many theories about what you should eat during an adventure race to optimize your performance as there are foods to choose from. One thing everyone agrees on—food, or lack thereof, affects your racing performance, so always pick foods you enjoy and will want to eat. Try a number of different things during your workouts and establish your own favorite list of foods for racing.

Theories on what to eat for endurance change with each new published report on the subject. There are many books that offer information on sports nutrition for maximum performance. This chapter presents a brief synopsis of some of the popular theories but does not go into detail on the scientific aspects of optimal nutrition. If you are interested in a more in-depth examination of nutrition and sports, check out Monique Ryan's *The Complete Guide to Sports Nutrition* (VeloPress,1999) and Ellen Coleman's *Eating for Endurance* (Bull Publishing Company, 1997).

In sprint adventure races of two to four hours, competitors will not need to eat much, perhaps only 100 to 200 calories during the entire race. Ingesting a few packets of gel or taking in liquid calories from an energy drink can easily accomplish this. In longer races, from twenty-four to thirty hours up to ten days, eating becomes critical to the success of each competitor and the team. During every day of racing, competitors can burn between 8,000 and 10,000 calories, but replenishing this quantity of food while racing is next to impossible. The best that competitors can do is try to consume a minimum of 300 to 400 calories per hour throughout the race. Even then, a calorie deficit will be established, but consuming anything more than 400 calories per hour is sometimes difficult for the human gut to absorb during heavy exercise (leading to cramping and other discomforts). Practice eating during training to get your system used to taking in calories while you are exerting yourself.

The average athlete carries enough fat in their body to provide fuel for many hours or even days—if they can efficiently access this energy. Adventure racers need to train their muscles to rely on fat for fuel in order to continue for longer periods of time. Muscles get their energy from a combination of fat and carbohydrates, but we are limited by the amount of carbohydrates our bodies can store. We can only store enough glycogen (which is how we stockpile carbohydrates for energy) to run about 20 miles—enough for a Hi-Tec adventure race but not enough for full-day or multiday races. Training for long periods, at an aerobic pace (typical of conditions in a long adventure race), will teach your muscles to increase their efficient use of fat.

What type of food is best to eat during an adventure race? The key is to keep your glycogen level up (from carbohydrates) or you will begin to tire and slow down dramatically. After ingestion, carbohydrates are broken down into simple sugars that are transported by the bloodstream to the liver, where they are converted to glucose. Some of this glucose is converted to glycogen and stored in muscles and the liver. Glucose from carbohydrates helps the muscles generate energy from fat. Therefore, make sure to take in at least 30 to 60 grams of carbohydrates per hour to maintain a basic supply. A standard sports bar has between 25 and 45 grams of carbohydrates. Proteins are also important during an endurance event. Early in exercise the body begins to break down the branched-chain amino acids (from protein) in the blood. Once these are no longer available from the blood, the body begins to burn muscle protein (the body eats its own muscle) to get at the acids it needs for energy. So continue to ingest enough protein during the race to prevent muscle breakdown (1.4 grams per kilogram of body weight, or roughly 60 to 80 grams of protein for most competitors per day). A typical sports bar contains 8 to 10 grams of protein; some protein bars on the market contain more than 20 grams of protein.

Probably the best advice for adventure racers is to take in a mix of carbohydrates, proteins, and fats throughout the race. In training, practice running slowly or hiking or biking after eating. When we started out in adventure racing, we were not used to exercising after eating, and rarely ate during exercise, so adventure racing was a big change. Now, after racing for several years, we can eat a little of almost anything and still exercise without any problem—a big plus in adventure racing. During periods of intense exercise, eating solid foods high in fat and protein can divert blood to the stomach for digestion and away from the muscles where it is needed. Therefore, during an adventure race, when the team is pushing hard, say, up a mountain, for example, this might be the time for liquid calories and gels instead of solid foods, which are harder to digest.

There are two main sources for food during an adventure race: foods you carry with you during the race and foods you eat at the transition area. In a longer race, food purchased from stores that you pass, or provided by people along the way can be a third source. One item that every team should carry during a long race is local currency! You never know when you will come across a convenience store or pizza parlor and want to get something to eat or drink. We have discovered in races around the world that you can probably get a Coca-Cola even in the most unlikely and remote places, and it might be just what the team needs to lift their spirits and make it to the finish line.

There are some basic considerations for choosing the foods you carry in an adventure race. You want to select foods that are calorie dense, light-weight, low volume, nonperishable, and not likely to melt if you are racing where it's warm.

Carry a combination of convenient food (energy bars and gels) and "real" food. Some examples of real food are:

▲ Gorp/trail mix
▲ Granola bars
▲ Chocolate, unless it will melt (Snickers and M&Ms are favorites, as well as malted milk balls, which are lightweight and calorie dense)
▲ Paydays or Salted Nut Rolls (if it's too hot for chocolate)
▲ Gummie Bears
▲ Fruit rollups
▲ Dried fruit
▲ Starbursts
▲ Beef/turkey jerky or salami sticks
▲ String cheese/Babybel cheese

▲ Pop Tarts (only carry the real deal, says Rebecca Rusch—no generic ones)

▲ Ritz Bitz (peanut butter and cheese)

FOOD AND ENTERTAINMENT

In the Raid Gauloises 2000 our team was able to get a meal from one of the mountain villages along the race route in Nepal. The family didn't speak any English but knew we were hungry and provided us with spicy ramen and beer. Afterward we thanked them by singing "American Pie" and "Twinkle, Twinkle Little Star" to their amusement and appreciation.

Both Rebecca Rusch and Robyn Benincasa, two of the best female adventure racers, claim that their secret weapon is Cheetos. Rebecca finds that she can always eat them, no matter how sick she feels. Pringles potato chips are another favorite with many racers. During the TV broadcast of Eco-Challenge 1997, the winning team of Andrea and Keith Murray, Robert Nagle, and John Howard were shown in TAs eating lots of Pringles. This sparked an extensive discussion among adventure racers on a popular Web chat list about the nutritional aspects of Pringles and speculation about why the best racers in the world were eating them. Finally, Robert Nagle stepped in and wrote, "We were eating Pringles because at that point in the race they tasted good—and anything that will go down easily adds calories, which is a good thing. End of story."

Will Burkhart of Team S.C.A.R. and, more recently, Team Explorer, says that a teammate introduced him to bags of mini-muffins during the Discovery Channel Adventure Race 2000 in New Zealand. He claimed it was like having home-baked banana bread handed to him in the middle of a race.

Don't be afraid to occasionally carry something that might be a little heavy (a sandwich, slice of cold pizza, or bean burrito) and eat it first to reduce the weight in your pack. Sometimes these little treats are literally what keep you going.

Our favorite treat during a long race is small Ziploc bags of dehydrated foods that you can add water to and eat while traveling (experiment with what works well in cold water). One of the favorite treats of Billy Mattison (captain of Team Vail, Eco-Challenge winners in 1998) is a granola-muesli mix sprinkled with powdered milk that he can simply add water to, and—voilà!—a bowl of cereal. Billy also likes to carry a small plastic jar in which he hydrates dry soup; a plastic spoon is attached to the outside of the lid with a string so that the jar and spoon are always together in his pack. Powdered soup, even mixed with cold water, can taste unbelievably good in the middle of a long race.

Other things you can put into Ziploc bags and rehydrate with water in the field are powdered mashed potatoes and powdered milk (with or without dried cheddar cheese or Parmesan cheese), couscous with dry spaghetti sauce, and Stove Top stuffing mix.

Rebecca Rusch of Team Atlas Snowshoe Rubicon (fourth at Eco-Challenge 1999) likes to crush dry ramen noodles and put them in a Ziploc with one-half of the flavor packet. Add water, wait, and eat! She also likes to add pieces of turkey jerky with the water for extra flavor.

Dehydrated food in Ziploc bags is great; just put water in the bag, wait fifteen to twenty minutes and it will be ready. Bite a hole in a corner of the baggie and suck the food out. This makes it easy to eat and walk at the same time.

Many competitors carry and eat MRE (Meal Ready-to-Eat), a high-calorie meal in a small pouch that can fit in your pocket. These are commonly used in the military; you either love them or you hate them. Although they aren't exactly lightweight (1.5 pounds), they pack a wallop in calories, have a very long shelf life, and are resistant to chemical and biological contamination, for what it's worth.

A good way to organize your food for a race lasting more than twelve hours is to place a variety of foods in large Ziploc bags. Each bag should contain what you will need for twenty-four hours (or make smaller bags for shorter races, such as six-hour bags for a twenty-four-to-thirty-hour race. Include a variety of foods that do not weigh a lot (careful, it can get heavy in a hurry!). Label each bag with your name so you or your support crew can find it quickly. This way, at each TA, you can grab the number of bags you think you will need for the upcoming section of the race.

According to Robyn Benincasa, during the Raid Gauloises 2000 and the Discovery Channel Adventure Race 2000, on the way to fourth- and third-place finishes respectively, the team ate a crunchy chocolate liquid concoction of Milo and powdered milk. Milo is a popular Australian product consisting of malt

A DAY'S WORTH OF FOOD

To replenish an 8,000-calorie loss per day during an adventure race would require approximately 40 energy bars, 80 gel packets, or 90 bananas. But that would be hard to enjoy, so here is an example of the twenty-four-hour, one-gallon Ziploc we carry:

> 4 energy bars (1,000 cal)
>
> 2 Go Sports powdered drinks (500 cal)
>
> 1 Nut Roll (250 cal)
>
> 2 Snickers Bars (500 cal)
>
> 2 bags couscous with spaghetti sauce (400 cal)
>
> 1 bag dry potatoes with cheese (250 cal)
>
> 1½ cups trail mix (500 cal)
>
> 5 gels (500 cal)
>
> 3 string cheese sticks (300 cal)
>
> 4 salami sticks and/or jerky (500 cal)

This results in nearly 5,000 calories, short of what is being expended, but a reasonable amount to carry and consume. Other items racers carry include:

▲ Chewing gum to keep the mouth moist and clean the teeth.

▲ Liquid calories in the form of powdered shakes (our favorite is Go! Sports—yummy! www.systemgo.com).

▲ Electrolyte packets, such as Emer'gen-C, and others.

Taking in some much-needed liquid calories.
© 2000 Liz Caldwell

extract cocoa, sugar, and vitamins and minerals, manufactured by Nestlé. They mixed it extra thick, passed it around, and were able to eat it even when nothing else would go down.

Strive to eat something every thirty minutes, or at least every hour, to continuously fuel the body. The key is to ingest small, consistent amounts to maintain optimal athletic performance. Practice this during your training efforts because it's not an easy thing to do.

A few things to remember about eating during the race:

1. It helps to have one team member remind everyone to eat every half hour or hour (set a watch timer).

2. If you are feeling good and notice that a teammate is not eating, get some food out and give them some of yours. Sometimes the effort of getting the food out is more than a tired teammate can handle, but they will eat what you offer and hopefully recover quickly.

3. Keep food readily accessible in waistband pockets and on the outside of the pack. When finished taking something from a Ziploc bag of food, put it back in a teammate's outside pack pocket so that the team doesn't have to stop.

IN THE TRANSITION

The time you spend in the TA is always important because it adds up quickly, but it is even more important in a short, sprint adventure race. For short races you will want to minimize the time spent in the TA, so grab food that you can eat quickly while getting ready for the next event. In a short race, competitors will most likely grab something to eat, such as a gel pack, on the way out of the TA.

In the longer races when you arrive in the TA, first drink, and then drink some more—energy drinks like Gatorade, bottled water, cola, juice—anything you can get your hands on. Then eat lots! Anything goes in the transition; this is the team's chance to replenish. If the race is supported, your support crew will be providing you with food while you prepare for the next event. Most racers

Resupplying from the gear box.
© 1998 Darrin Eisman

look forward to a variety of foods including:

Pasta (with meatballs, chicken, cheese)

Mashed potatoes with butter and cheese

Hard-boiled eggs with salt

Chips of all kinds

Burritos (bean and meat)

Soup or stew

Rice with meat, veggies, cheese

Grilled cheese sandwiches

Tuna sandwiches with mayonnaise, cheese

One of the first things we do in the TA is drink a can of a high-calorie beverage, such as ENSURE Plus, a quick source of 360 calories. Many teams rely on dehydrated foods, such as Mountain House or Alpine Aire, for a variety of quick foods including scrambled eggs, pasta, stews, and more. In unsupported races, each competitor will have additional food and special treats stored in their gear box.

The food you eat in transition should not be spicy (unless you have tried it in training) and should include meat or other protein. Fruit is a wonderful treat—melon, banana, kiwi, oranges—anything with juice and easy to get down (apples are not easy to eat in transition). During one seven-day race, our support crew managed to have hamburgers and fries waiting for us at the TA. It didn't matter that they were cold; they were the best hamburgers we'd ever eaten. Other teams have been spotted enjoying pizza during the transition.

HYDRATION

Almost nothing is more important in any athletic event than proper hydration. It is essential both in a short sprint adventure race and in a multiday race. We all know, or have read, that dehydration leads to poor performance, and we know that dehydration is one of the leading causes of competitors dropping out in adventure races.

Competitors lose water through respiration and sweat, and even more water is lost at high altitudes with low humidity. Dehydration reduces blood volume and increases blood viscosity, resulting in decreased flow of oxygen and nutrients to the muscles, reduced removal of carbon dioxide and lactic acid, and reduced circulation to the extremities. All of these effects are detrimental in adventure racing.

The symptoms of dehydration include muscle cramping, fatigue, rapid heart rate, and shortness of breath. More advanced stages of dehydration can lead to vomiting, hot, dry skin, coma, and death.

How much water do you need? The simple answer is: a lot. Competitors need to consistently drink small quantities to maintain optimal performance. That said, there is a life-threatening condition called hyponatremia that can occur when too much water is consumed without replacing the sodium typically

STAYING HYDRATED

How much water or fluid will you need? This will depend on many factors including your gender, genetics, acclimation to the altitude, as well as the temperature and humidity level. Here is one method for estimating your particular needs. Try them during training:

1. Weigh yourself before training (kilograms) (urinate before weighing).
2. Keep track of liquids (in liters) consumed during exercise.
3. Note the length of time that you exercise.
4. Weigh yourself again after exercise.
5. Subtract postexercise weight from pre-exercise weight (for example, 59 kilograms – 58 kilograms = 1 kilogram = 1 liter).
6. Add the number of liters consumed during exercise (for example, 1 liter [from #5 above] + 1 liter consumed = 2 liters).
7. Divide the resulting number of liters by the time (hours) exercised. Therefore, if you ran for two hours, your liquid requirement is 1 liter (24 ounces) for each hour of exercise.

lost in endurance events. Drinking only water can dilute the already low amounts of sodium in the blood, resulting in fatigue, weakness, cramping, nausea, vomiting, bloating, puffiness in the face and fingers, dizziness, headache, fainting and unconsciousness, coma, and sometimes death. Symptoms of hyponatremia can occur during a race or after and can be confused with dehydration. This condition can be avoided by consuming sports drinks at TAs and occasionally during the race. We always carry electrolyte replacement packets. Our favorite that we swear by is Emer'gen-C; it's lightweight and tasty (for more on dehydration, see Chapter 14, "Injury and Illness").

A typical hydration bladder holds 80 to 100 ounces. You will probably need to refill it every four to five hours to stay hydrated throughout the race. It is helpful to take several hydration bladders with you to a race so that in the TA you can quickly replace your empty one with a prefilled one. In a short race, particularly in the summer, you might even want to keep your replacement bladders in a cooler to keep the water nice and cold.

Breakfast at sunrise.
© 1999 Dan Campbell

Many competitors forget to eat and drink enough during a race, resulting in failure for themselves and their team. Don't let it happen to you. Eat even when a bar makes you gag, drink before you get thirsty, and replenish your electrolytes through food, sports drinks, or electrolyte capsules.

CHAPTER 14

INJURY
AND
ILLNESS

© 2000 Dan Campbell

Unfortunately, at one time or another, almost every adventure racer will be afflicted with some kind of injury or debilitation that can affect their training and racing. If it happens to you during a race, and depending on the severity, it can mean the end of the race for you and your team. Injury prevention during a race, then, becomes paramount. The most common "injuries" that can result in a competitor dropping out of an adventure race include dehydration, foot problems, hypothermia, and knee injuries. Other injuries that are less common but occasionally seen in adventure races include separated shoulders, sprained ankles, severe cuts, eye injuries, and bee and other insect stings or bites.

In the Eco-Challenge 2000 one competitor suffered a punctured lung resulting from a fall from his mountain bike, and another had to drop out early in the race after a leech attached itself to her eye and caused complications. These were unusual injuries, yet it reminds us that almost any kind of injury is possible when we participate in adventure sports. Fortunately, serious injuries rarely happen during adventure races, partly because of the extreme safety measures taken by race directors.

DEHYDRATION

The importance of proper hydration and electrolyte balance was mentioned in the prior chapter on food. Competitors lose water primarily through respiration and sweat. During heavy exertion, racers can lose 1 to 3 liters of water per hour through sweat. The combination of extreme cold temperatures and altitude common in an adventure race can dramatically increase the rate of water loss through the lungs (respiration).

Checking on a teammate.
© 1997 Dan Campbell

Along with taking in adequate quantities of water, competitors need to replace electrolytes lost in respiration and sweat to avoid heat exhaustion. Heat exhaustion is not a life-threatening illness, but symptoms can include fatigue, exhaustion, nausea, lightheadedness, and possibly heat cramps. Fluids may have been replaced but not the electrolytes. Heat exhaustion can often be treated rapidly with the ingestion of an electrolyte solution such as Emer'gen-C and rest in a shaded place.

Electrolyte imbalances can lead to a perilous drop in sodium levels in the blood, a condition called hyponatremia. Hyponatremia causes fatigue, weakness, cramping, nausea, vomiting, bloating, fainting, pulmonary edema, seizures, coma, and sometimes death. To prevent dehydration and hyponatremia, drink plenty of fluids, and especially fluids that will replace sodium and other electrolytes, and eat salty foods periodically during the race or take capsules containing essential electrolytes. Sports drinks typically contain between 120 and 430 milligrams of sodium per liter, which is far short of the amount of sodium per liter in sweat (700 and 1,100 milligrams). Some racers simply add a small amount of salt to their hydration bladder or sport drink to boost the sodium (but not enough to affect the taste) or pour salt into their hand and lick it off.

The electrolyte capsule we take during long training sessions and races is Succeed! Buffer/Electrolyte Caps from Succeed! Sportsdrink, Inc., with 350 milligrams of sodium and 21 milligrams of potassium. Many adventure racers and ultrarunners experience nausea and even vomiting during prolonged effort. The chemical buffering system in Succeed! Caps neutralizes the stomach acids formed during exercise, which in turn reduces the nausea often associated with exercise in the heat. Other popular electrolyte capsules include E-Caps from Hammer Nutrition and Endurox from GNC.

Eating salty foods (chips, nuts) during the race will help to keep the sodium in balance. Maintaining your electrolyte levels will also help to prevent swelling of your hands and feet, which can reduce the occurrence of blisters on the feet and allow you to get your bike shoes on for the next leg of the race! The bottom line for adventure racers regarding dehydration is to drink well before you are thirsty, and take in electrolytes.

FOOT PROBLEMS

Foot problems are the bane of almost every adventure racer sooner or later. A great deal of information about foot care, on both prevention and treatment, is provided in a book by John Vonhof titled *Fixing Your Feet: Prevention and Treatment for Athletes, 2nd Edition* (Footwork Publications, 2000). The prevention of foot problems is probably the most important aspect of foot care. Try a variety of things in training; know what to do to prevent blisters and how to care for them. Watching elite adventure racer John Howard, with victories too numerous to list, drop out of the Eco-Challenge 2000 because of trashed feet was heartbreaking. Seeing him hobble around after the race, using a chair as a walker, was a reminder that even the best racers can be surprised by foot problems occasionally.

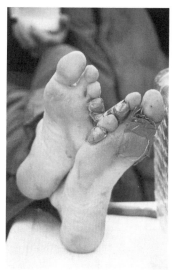

Using duct tape for blister care.
© 1995 Dan Campbell

Blisters, those little fluid-filled nightmares, are caused by friction, either from rubbing occurring inside a shoe or sock, or from grit trapped in the shoe, and they are exacerbated when combined with wet conditions and excessive heat. The winning team at the ELF Authentic Adventure Race 2000 in

Brazil attributed their win, in part, to the good care they took of their feet. During rest stops of more than one minute, they took their shoes off to let their feet air-dry and propped their legs up to reduce swelling. Most team members also slathered their feet with Betadine antiseptic to prevent foot fungus, and a silicone-based cream to prevent friction.

Frequent sock changes will also help to keep the feet dry and reduce the chance of blisters forming. The choice of sock used in the race can also have an impact on how well the feet will hold up. Our entire team wore socks containing Teflon fibers by Blister Guard during the Eco-Challenge 2000 and had some of the best feet in the race. Other people swear by a two-layer system of socks: a thin inner liner covered by (in wet conditions) a SealSkinz Waterblocker sock. Cathy Sassin used this system successfully while winning the ELF 2000. We've also seen adventure racers apply an antiperspirant deodorant to their feet in an effort to prevent moisture buildup.

Many adventure racers, us included, spend time toughening their feet prior to a race. Beginning about a month before the race, we begin to use a product called Tuffoot—originally designed to toughen dogs' paws but now made for humans—combined with nightly foot soaks in a mixture of Betadine and tea (see *Fixing Your Feet*) or applications of tincture of benzoin. Be prepared for your feet to become a little orange and very dry . . . if not tough!

Two of the most popular techniques used by adventure racers to prevent blisters during the race are the use of lubricants (Hydropel, Avon Silicone Glove, BodyGlide, Bag Balm) and taping. Lubricants need to be reapplied frequently; whenever the team stops, everyone should air-dry their feet and reapply the lubricant, if possible. Taping is a great proactive and preventative measure against blisters, especially if you have a history of blisters. The tape will not stick well or stay in place without first applying some kind of tape adhesive, such as tincture of benzoin (our favorite), Tuffner spray, or Tuf-Skin. Let the adherent dry slightly, then put tape (we use duct tape) smoothly over the areas that usually blister. *Fixing Your Feet* provides a superb description and shows diagrams of the various methods of taping.

Once a blister occurs, what can you do? During a race it is best to:

1. Drain the fluid from the blister, leaving the outer skin intact.
2. Apply antibiotic ointment, such as Neosporin, to the ruptured blister to help prevent infection.

3. Apply tape adhesive, such as tincture of benzoin, around the blister. Be careful—tincture of benzoin will really hurt if you get it in the blister.

4. Cover the blister with a cushioning bandage: Compeed or Blister Relief, moleskin, adhesive felt, or whatever you know works for you. (Compeed is made with an elastic polyurethane film over a moisture-absorbing and adhering layer that works well for us. It stays on for several days and allows us to continue the race in relative comfort.)

5. Cover the blister product with a wrapping of duct tape, or, if the treatment is extensive, wrap the foot in a self-adhesive Coban tape so that everything will stay in place longer.

We carry sealed hypodermic needles in our first-aid kit so that we can puncture and drain any blisters. Billy Mattison of Team Vail keeps a safety pin attached to the lanyard of his compass around his neck for the same purpose and quick access during rest stops.

Some of the more extreme methods of blister care that we have encountered at races include the injection of tincture of benzoin directly into the drained blister to seal it shut (very painful) and the use of Super Glue in the same manner. *Fixing Your Feet* recommends against the use of Super Glue, but no reason is given. Many adventure racers have used Super Glue successfully to get through a race.

Other common foot problems include soggy feet and resulting fissures, and fungal infections. In races where the feet are constantly wet, it becomes critical to find opportunities to let them air-dry. When the foot becomes overly

MEDICAL ASSISTANCE DURING RACES

A medical staff is usually available at the transition to treat serious medical problems. Occasionally, medical staff will even bathe and cleanse your feet (pure heaven) or treat blisters and preventatively wrap your feet to ward off blisters. Historically, this is more true at the Eco-Challenge, while the Raid Gauloises medical staff is more likely to just treat serious foot problems. At the Raid Gauloises, teams are expected to care for their own feet, unless it is very severe.

soft and white from constant moisture, there is a danger that the skin will begin to peel off in sheets. Painful fissures may occur in the skin; they need to be treated as a blister or sealed shut with a product like Super Glue. During the Raid Gauloises 2000, our team took their shoes and socks off while paddling during the rafting sections to air-dry the feet. Just be sure to secure your shoes to the boat so that they won't be washed overboard!

A final note on blisters and bad feet: Use trekking poles on the hiking sections, especially ones with significant elevation gain and loss. Trekking poles can reduce the weight placed on the feet by up to 30 percent.

HYPOTHERMIA

Hypothermia is caused by exposure to cold and aggravated by wet, wind, and exhaustion. It is defined as the body's failure to maintain a temperature of 97°F. The moment your body begins to lose heat faster than it produces it, you are undergoing exposure. As a result, your body makes involuntary adjustments, like shivering, to preserve normal temperature in the vital organs.

Most hypothermia cases develop in air temperatures between 30° and 50°F. Dehydration and lack of food and rest increase the risk of hypothermia. Exposure greatly reduces your normal endurance. You may think you are doing fine, but the only thing preventing you from going into hypothermia is that you are moving. If you stop, however brief, your rate of body heat production instantly drops by 50 percent or more, and you may begin shivering violently almost immediately.

To avoid hypothermia:

▲ Stay dry—wet clothes lose about 90 percent of their insulating value.

▲ Beware of the wind; even a slight breeze carries heat away from bare skin much faster than still air and refrigerates wet clothes by evaporating moisture from the surface.

▲ Reduce the amount of heat lost to exhalation by covering the mouth and nose area with wool or a bandana.

▲ Wear clothing that can be ventilated or taken off and that will not absorb water but will breathe.

▲ Wear clothing that will keep you warm even if it is wet.

▲ Don't sit on the ground, or snow—heat will rapidly be lost through conduction.

Persistent or violent shivering is a clear warning that you are on the verge of hypothermia. Watch yourself and your teammates for symptoms:

Uncontrollable fits of shivering

Vague, slow, slurred speech

Memory lapses or incoherence

Immobile, fumbling hands

Frequent stumbling

Drowsiness (to sleep is to die)

Apparent exhaustion

You can slip into hypothermia in a matter of minutes. If it happens to a teammate, get them into dry clothing and wrap them in an emergency blanket covering the head and neck. Try to get them to drink to replace lost fluids. If needed, use your own body heat to warm your teammate.

During the inaugural FogDog 24-Hour Adventure Race in 2000 the race started with an ocean paddle in chilly water and with strong winds. The battle for most teams became one of trying to avoid hypothermia. Team Balance Bar (winners of the Hi-Tec Adventure Race series in 2000) had to drop out of the race only hours into it when one of their team members became severely hypothermic.

KNEE INJURIES

Knee injuries are the other most common "show-stopping" injuries around. Traveling over rough terrain and on steep descents, many racers end up with debilitating knee pain and swollen knees, which can quickly put an end to their race. Again, the use of poles can do a lot to prevent knee injuries by absorbing the shock in the steep uphill and downhill trekking sections, which reduces stress to your knees and lower back. When hiking with poles, you maintain a more upright posture, even when carrying a pack, allowing for more efficient breathing and increased endurance.

When knee pain first begins to appear, don't hesitate to let the rest of the team know and ask for help getting extra weight off of your back. Use trekking poles if you have them, and if you don't, find a walking stick or two. Try

SAFE FOOD

Our Raid Gauloises 2000 team elected to take all of the food we needed to eat, before and during the race, with us to Tibet. We did not eat any of the food at the hotels we stayed in, or the food provided at the pre-race meeting. While many other teams became ill, we did not. It was not an easy solution, requiring self-restraint and determination as well as the additional cost of transporting many pounds of food to Tibet. We felt that in the end it was worth the effort.

taking ibuprofen to reduce the swelling and the pain. However, remember that ibuprofen can mask pain from a problem that, if not corrected, could have severe consequences later. (A list of typical team and individual first-aid kit requirements is presented in Appendix A).

OTHER AILMENTS

Beyond the most common injuries discussed, abdominal cramping occasionally afflicts competitors during adventure races, especially those races taking place in foreign countries. At the Raid Gauloises 2000 some team members did not even start the race due to gastrointestinal distress likely caused by ingestion of contaminated food or water.

Water obtained on the racecourse from streams, lakes, or any other source is potentially contaminated and should be treated chemically to disinfect it and remove the possibility of getting sick. Many racers use iodine tablets to chemically treat their water, though it is possible to develop a sensitivity to iodine over time. Iodine also can have an unpleasant taste, making it difficult to drink enough and stay hydrated. The iodine taste can be neutralized with vitamin C or a commercial product called Potable Aqua PA, but care must be taken not to add neutralizers to the water too soon, because they can affect the iodine's ability to disinfect the water. Use of iodine also requires a waiting period. If the water is cold, the recommended time can be as long as thirty minutes.

Another chemical treatment option for adventure racers is the use of dilute solutions of chlorine bleach (up to 8 milligrams per liter of water with optimal conditions). When using household chlorine bleach of 4 percent to 6 percent available chlorine, use two drops of bleach (0.05 milliliter per drop) for every quart liter of clear water, and four drops for cold or cloudy water. After adding the drops of chlorine bleach, shake and let stand for 30 minutes or, if the water is very cold or cloudy, for several hours. It is important to note that chlorine, when used in these amounts, is ineffective in killing giardia in very cold water, or water with a high concentration of suspended organic material such as mud. There are also products on the market (especially in Europe) that are similar to iodine but do not have the taste problem.

Ah, water . . .
© 1995 Dan Campbell

One of the best water treatment options for racing is the use of water bottles with filter systems built right in. Some of these systems, such as the Seychelle bottles, have filters that are impregnated with iodine to kill even the smallest organisms, such as viruses. If the bottle, such as the one made by SafeWater, has a pre-filter at the filling stage so much the better, because many of the water sources encountered in a race will be heavy with suspended dirt, which will clog up the treatment filter.

Avoid spreading germs among the team—difficult but not impossible. Carry and use a hand sanitizer or baby wipes, especially after defecating to prevent getting sick. If someone on the team does get diarrhea, a dose or two of over-the-counter anti-diarrhea medicine will hopefully take care of it, unless it is something more serious that requires medical attention.

All cuts should be treated with antibiotic ointment (usually a required item in your first-aid kit), especially when racing in a foreign country. While racing in New Zealand and Brazil, we ended up with infected cuts everywhere, and the ones on the hands were especially painful when trying to paddle!

Competitors who wear contact lenses have the additional concern of cleanliness when removing and replacing their lenses. Many competitors use extended-wear lenses, but some are not able to and as a result may have to carry special cleaning solutions and storage cases. We both wore contact lenses, but because of the amount of racing we do, we decided to undergo LASIK eye surgery. This has been particularly helpful in several races that had us swimming in whitewater. It was a relief not to be worried about trying to finish the race after losing a contact lens. Those who do race wearing contacts might consider carrying an extra pair of lenses or glasses in the event one gets lost during the race.

Snowblindness, or burned eyes, is another concern, especially when racing at high altitudes and on snow. Good sunglasses are a must. Isaac Wilson of Team Eco-Internet lost his sunglasses in one race and ended up fashioning emergency goggles from duct tape and adding narrow eye slits. Unfortunately, he still ended up with an annoying case of mild snowblindness, with irritated, teary eyes.

Sores can develop in the mouth during the long races because of the types of food competitors consume. This is partly due to the imbalance of electrolytes and lack of nutrients that develops over time during the race. We have found that the use of electrolyte capsules help in the prevention of this affliction. One former teammate insisted that consistently brushing his teeth and/or chewing gum also helped prevent this problem. Unfortunately when it does happen, eating becomes uncomfortable.

Many adventure racers and ultrarunners experience nausea and even vomiting during prolonged exercise. Sodium depletion may not be the single cause of nausea in endurance athletes. The foods that we eat normally are sodium overloaded, so the more likely culprit is a combination of many things, including depletion of potassium and low blood sugar. The most common causes of nausea and vomiting are probably related to problems from dehydration and lack of blood flow to the gut. While racing, our muscles demand extra blood flow, which is robbed from the stomach. As a result it is not uncommon to experience gut cramping and even diarrhea during a race. Undigested foods (if you have ingested a lot of food, or foods that are tough to digest, like jerky) just sit in your stomach. Excess acid begins to build up, resulting in abdominal cramps, bloating, nausea, and vomiting. Another factor potentially contributing to nausea and vomiting is hyperthermia, or overheating of the body. This can also be related to dehydration, as proper hydration helps to keep the body core temperature from getting too high.

Many adventure races take place at high altitudes. The effects of altitude sickness can be serious, so if the race you compete in is taking place at a high altitude, take the time to become familiar with the effects and symptoms to watch for in yourself and your teammates. Many competitors were adversely affected by altitude at the Raid Gauloises 2000 in Tibet, which went to almost 17,000 feet, and dropped out of the race. At the Mild Seven Outdoor Quest 2000, competitors were required to carry bags of oxygen during one of the mountain climbs. Although we live and train at altitude in Colorado, we used the oxygen in order to get rid of it and make it easier to carry. It provided a tremendous boost, and none of the competitors in the race experienced altitude problems.

A sensitive subject in adventure racing today is the part that drugs play. There are competitors who openly choose to use performance-enhancing drugs that would be banned in other sports. The Eco-Challenge 2000 was the first race to prohibit drugs and institute random drug testing among competitors. The list of banned substances was based on the International Olympic Committee's list, with some additional substances added from National Sporting Organizations. The list included stimulants, such as:

Ephedrine

Pseudoephedrine

Phenylephrine

Amphetamines

Ecstasy

Caffeine (in excess)

The complete list of banned substances also included anabolic agents; diuretics; narcotics or substances such as cocaine, TCH, alcohol, morphine, heroin, methadone, beta blockers, sedatives; and peptide and glycoprotein hormones, such as erythropoetin (EPO) and human growth hormone (HGH). Many racers utilize energy boosters, such as Ripped Fuel, that contain the herb ma huang (ephedra), a naturally occurring form of ephedrine, and caffeine to combat the drowsiness that occurs during multiday races. These substances were banned from use at Eco-Challenge. The effort by Eco-Challenge to eliminate the use of drugs during races is commendable but very difficult to police.

Fighting sleepiness is one of the most difficult aspects of long adventure races. If the entire team is fighting the "sleep monster" it might be best to simply stop and sleep for twenty to thirty minutes. A short nap can be enough to rejuvenate everyone; at other times a longer sleep might be required. Many racers eat some chocolate-covered coffee beans, in the hope that the caffeine will wake them up. Others use chewing tobacco to get that late night boost. Homeopathic products have been made specifically for use in adventure races, including one called Sleep Monster (HCH Sports Formulas of New Zealand), which is advertised to fight drowsiness and disorientation from lack of sleep. It does not contain any stimulants.

Hallucinations are a common experience in long adventure races where competitors become sleep deprived. Robyn Benincasa was seen having some great conversations with bushes and trees during the night in Eco-Challenge 1999. It happens—and probably the only real cure is to sleep.

People getting ready to try their first adventure race often ask if they should practice sleep deprivation. Sleep deprivation is never pleasant and it isn't likely that you can train yourself to not experience its effects, so there is no need to put yourself through it until it happens. Save it for the race. Just know that you will feel better as soon as the sun begins to come up.

AFTEREFFECTS

There can be many aftereffects from adventure racing. The threat of contracting a disease when racing in a third world country is real. Competitors are responsible for making sure that they have all of the required inoculations for travel and should research the area they will be racing in to see what additional precautions they can take. One of the unpleasant and highly publicized aftereffects for many participants in the Eco-Challenge 2000 was the occurrence of leptospirosis, a bacterial infection, most likely picked up from swimming in recently flooded waters. Unfortunately, many competitors found themselves getting very sick and even requiring hospitalization after returning home from the race.

For the Raid Gauloises 2000 teams were required to carry prescription medicine including antibiotics, altitude sickness medication, and asthma medication. Some physicians are reluctant to prescribe this medication because the competitors will be determining what medication to take without the benefit of the knowledge of a physician's assessment. Many adventure racers carry at a minimum prescription antibiotics, in the event of an infection.

We recommend that you take a basic first-aid course if you plan to participate in adventure racing, or even if you just plan to become more active in the outdoors. Having at least one person on your team who knows what to do in an emergency is an advantage and safety factor for everyone.

As we noted in the prior chapter, it is nearly impossible to take in as many calories as are expended during the race. How much weight will a competitor lose as a result? That depends on many factors including the amount of calories consumed and expended, and genetics. Ian Adamson lost close to 20 pounds while racing in ELF 1999. For the average racer a loss of between 5 and 10 pounds in a seven-day race is common. Once the race is over, though, the body responds with a ravenous appetite, storing up calories in case it is "starved" again, so if you aren't careful, you can end up weighing more than you did when you started the race!

Often after the race is over, the extremities will swell—to the point where it is sometimes difficult to see where the ankle is! This is probably due to a combination of waste products and the end result of electrolyte imbalances produced during the race. Staying hydrated during the race can help to prevent this aftereffect. Other lingering effects can include numbness or tingling in the feet, probably a result of the extreme stress on the feet and impingement on the nerves, but it will eventually wear off. Toenails may also have been bruised and become blackened and fall off.

One of the unexpected aftereffects of racing for first-time racers is the slight feeling of depression that can follow the attainment of a large goal. Take a break from training, do things with friends and family, and the depression will lift—then you will be ready to begin training for your next race!

AFTERWORD

THE
FUTURE
OF
ADVENTURE
RACING

© 1999 Dan Campbell

Adventure racing, while considered one of the fastest-growing team sports of the 1990s, is still in its infancy. Where has the sport been and where is it going? Having "officially" begun in 1989, though actually much earlier in its rough form in the 1970s in New Zealand, the sport began well after the popularity of mountain biking, distance running, and triathlon. In the early days, the term "adventure racing" was coined to describe the few multisport endurance team events lasting many days (Raid Gauloises and Eco-Challenge). Today, we see the term expanded and applied in the media to a wide variety of events, ranging from solo endurance events such as the Iditarod Race in Alaska and the XTERRA off-road triathlon series, to two-hour team sprint races. As we look ahead, we wonder: How will the sport of adventure racing change and evolve? What changes will we see in racing and races? How will the competitors change?

The sport of adventure racing will continue to grow and evolve, with the United States continuing to make its mark on the sport. For the first decade of its existence, adventure racing has been an unregulated and nonstandardized sport. This has been considered fine by most countries and competitors and is even thought to be consistent with the adventure concept of the sport. In the United States, however, the movement toward establishing a "governing body" has led to the creation of at least two organizations as of early 2001: USA Adventure Racing (USAAR) and the United States Adventure Racing Association (USARA).

The USAAR headed by Michael Epstein Sports Productions, was originally established to provide standardization for the sprint Hi-Tec type race series but it is now broadening its scope. The USARA currently provides race "sanctioning" similar to the USA Triathlon federation sanctioning of triathlon races in the United States. The emphasis of both associations is on establishing credibility for its events through requiring minimum safety standards and providing insurance packages for the events' management groups. Similar to USA Triathlon, competitors are charged a fee to join the association and race in the "sanctioned," or participating, races. It is interesting that concern over standardizing races and establishing a governing body exists primarily in the United States. The Europeans, Aussies, and Kiwis, who started the sport, have expressed no desire or need to form a governing body.

From New Zealand to Europe to the United States, adventure racing has grown all over the world. It has been the appeal to many to be able to visit and experience such "foreign lands." This has led to the introduction of the sport to many new arenas, such that adventure racing has become quite visible and popular in Japan, China, Brazil, and Africa, just to name a few more recent "converts." It is this growth and exposure internationally that will continue to fuel the expansion of the sport worldwide.

Adventure races will continue to come and go as the sport grows. Some will be cancelled due to lack of sponsorship or other reasons, while others will take root and continue to shape the future of the sport, In fact, this growth may ultimately lead to the need for an international committee to better coordinate and develop races around the world. In addition, as the sport is popularized and finds itself growing further and further away from its roots, we may even see an interest in it gaining status as an Olympic sport. All of this will only be attained through national organizations in each country, as well as an international group working for overall coordination and direction. This may be years away, which most today would think is a good thing. However, coordination among the major adventure races in the world is something that many believe is needed now. In 2001, the Raid Gauloises, the Eco-Challenge, the Mild Seven Outdoor Quest, and the Southern Traverse occur within just six weeks of each other. Either the strong will survive and others will weaken, or a coordinated effort will be undertaken.

Attempts have been made in the past to develop magazines devoted strictly to adventure racing, but with little success. Race coverage will continue to grow in publications devoted to the more mainstream disciplines of running, paddling, climbing, and triathlon, as well as in more general adventure and outdoor magazines. The impact of the sport on marketing will continue because of the dramatic images produced from the races, and the adventure travel market will continue to grow, too, as more and more people see adventure races and want to try a "tame" and controlled version of the sport. "Adventure" has become a catch word for millions of Americans, and its importance can be seen in the success of the recent TV and film productions *Survivor* and *Castaway* that glorify the idea of adventure and challenge in the wilderness.

We can also anticipate more television coverage of adventure racing. In 1996 the Eco-Challenge burst onto the media scene with extraordinary television coverage by the Discovery Channel for the British Columbia race. The Discovery Channel continued with annual Eco-Challenge broadcasts through 1999; in 2000 Eco-Challenge Productions' Mark Burnett signed a new agreement with USA Network for coverage of the Eco-Challenge 2000 in Borneo. As a result, the Discovery Channel—now split from coverage of the Eco-Challenge—formed a new partnership with Geoff Hunt and his Southern Traverse race in New Zealand for coverage of the Southern Traverse 2000 (called the Discovery Channel Adventure Race). As such, 2001 is the first year that two major expedition-length adventure races—Eco-Challenge and the Discovery Channel Adventure Race—will receive broad market coverage in the United States, and as this continues, so will interest in the sport. Other races such as Hi-Tec and the Mild Seven Outdoor Quest also have strong television coverage, but they have not yet had the impact that Eco-Challenge has had, particularly in the United States.

Television coverage is vital to the growth and success of adventure racing, as this is what attracts sponsors, which ultimately helps make the events more affordable for competitors and race directors alike. Successful television broadcasts and sponsorships also allow for greater prize money opportunity. The Mild Seven Outdoor Quest, since its inception, has offered the most lucrative purse in the sport ($200,000 in 2001), with the Eco-Challenge and the Discovery Channel Adventure Race just behind. To date, there has not been significant prize money in most of the shorter races or race series. Yet one would expect that to change; in fact, the inaugural FogDog 24-Hour Adventure Race offered a top prize of $10,000 in 2000, and the Wild Onion Urban Adventure Race is offering $25,000 in prize money in 2001. With more and stronger athletes getting into adventure racing, money will lure the top teams and competitors, and television and sponsors will ultimately support competition among the best. In addition, shorter events offer closer and, in some respects, more exciting racing for the viewers, as well as reduced production costs. We may also see more races like the Mild Seven Outdoor Quest—fast, stage races—where top athletes face each other for shorter, consecutive days of all-out racing. One way or the other, expect to see more adventure racing on television, complete with higher stakes.

The Internet has been the leading communicator for the sport and will likely remain so for years to come. The presence of adventure racing on the Internet is well established and can be used to link competitors and races from around the world with ease.

How will races and racing change in the future? It is probable that we will see more shorter races, urban races, and "fun" races; greater variety in team configurations (including solo); more series races and championships; and more stage races.

Races of shorter distances will continue to surface across the United States and throughout the world. These not only allow more people to get a taste for the sport but, also, make such racing possible for those with a full-time job or schedule (expedition-length races typically will require three to four weeks of time just to do the race).

The shorter races, and even many longer ones, are beginning to have less reliance on the aspect of navigation as a means to get through the course. Many adventure races now use mostly marked courses, where racers are required to stay on the defined course. Navigation has often been the limiting factor for most teams in adventure racing, and removing this element will certainly continue to change the face of the sport, allowing more people to give it a try.

Additionally, we will see adventure racing in urban areas grow, making the sport accessible to large areas of population. While these events may not have the "wilderness" feel, they can certainly be an adventure and allow competitors to experience everyday locations in a much different way (like rappelling down the side of a tall building). Additional "fun" races, such as the Muddy Buddy race series in the United States, designed for teams of two to get muddy and have fun, will continue to be created. And the military will continue to make its mark on adventure racing, with the advent of races limited to people who serve or have served in the military.

Stage races will also grow within the sport of adventure racing. Building off the format and success of the Mild Seven Outdoor Quest, these types of races allow teams to experience a variety of disciplines, racing in challenging and new terrain, while not pushing the limit on sleep deprivation or nighttime exposure.

We hope to see the development and expansion of what we call "Junior Adventure Challenges." We produced such an experience in 1998 in Winter Park, Colorado, for kids aged seven to fourteen. Individually, the participants biked a short distance to a pond, joined with two other "racers," paddled a canoe around the pond a couple of times, returned to the start on their bike, completed a fun "orienteering" section in a nearby treed area, and finished the challenge on a climbing wall. It was forty-five to sixty minutes of pure fun and adventure for the kids and their parents. It was also a great introduction to a multisport activity, and a first exposure for many to some of the disciplines. There is a definite opportunity for a similar event series to help get our youth into the outdoors.

Everywhere in the world there is a growth in "race series" complete with a championship race at the end of the series. The Salomon X-Adventure Race series held in locations around the world, the Adventure Concepts Florida Race Series and the Cal-Eco Race series in the United States are examples. The USARA has put together a series of existing races to form a "national championship" adventure race series, and the Hi-Tec Adventure Racing Series has its own championship. The Discovery Channel and Southern Traverse have established a seven-race "world championship" series in 2001.

How will competitors be different in the future? The early days of adventure racing definitely saw a domination of seasoned veterans being quite successful, particularly in the longer events. In fact, most of the top finishing teams in the expedition-length races of the 1990s typically included competitors in their late thirties to mid-forties. Robert Nagle, Ian Adamson, John Howard, and Jane Hall were examples of these successful "elder statesmen and -women" of the sport throughout the 1990s. Their success and the success of other mature competitors led many to tout the value of a long-term endurance base, maturity, and experience as they translate to stronger interpersonal skills and the ability to handle the sport mentally. In other words, their maturity and experience in endurance racing has better prepared them for the physical and mental rigors of adventure racing and they handle team aspects better.

More recently we have begun to see the success of younger, faster competitors in the sport, such as Team Nokia Adventure of Finland. Nokia, led by extraordinary adventure racer Petri Forsman, won the Mild Seven Outdoor Quest in 2000 with an average team age of twenty-six, as well as the Raid Gauloises that same year with an average age just slightly higher. These young athletes continue to push the sport; where competitors used to hike sections of long races, we now see them running. We will definitely see a proliferation of "younger" people in the sport and, while adventure racing will still be fueled by a more mature following, we will see an ever increasing number of races won by teams in their twenties and early thirties. We may even see the day of a "master's division" in adventure racing . . . that is, if us older folks get too frustrated! In 2001, for the first time, the Mild Seven Outdoor Quest is allowing teams to be either coed or include one male team member over the age of fifty.

As the sport evolves and provides a variety of races, more women will take up the challenge and try adventure racing. As a result, the gear and clothing industry will hopefully begin to respond and design more gender-specific items for adventure racing.

Adventure racing began in a loose, carefree, adventurous way. With television and other media exposure, together with people's yearning for excitement and challenge, the sport has grown tremendously. We certainly anticipate continued growth, probably at an exponential level, but we fervently hope that the sport's "loose, carefree, adventurous" roots have been solidly placed to remain forever.

APPENDIX A

MANDATORY GEAR FOR ADVENTURE RACING

Examples of the gear and safety equipment required for some adventure races are provided below. If you plan to do one of the following races, please contact the race directors to obtain the official race information and required gear list. Lists included here are MountainQuest Adventure Races, the Salomon X-Adventure Race (North America), the Eco-Challenge Adventure Race, and the Raid Gauloises.

MOUNTAINQUEST ADVENTURE RACES

MANDATORY TEAM GEAR (TO BE CARRIED AT ALL TIMES DURING THE RACE)

▲ Water purification system (filter, iodine, bleach), enough for the whole team

▲ 1 compass

▲ 1 survival mirror

▲ 1 knife

- ▲ 1 team first-aid kit
- ▲ 1 shovel for burying human waste
- ▲ 1 lighter or waterproof matches
- ▲ 1 emergency strobe light (visible for up to 3 miles)

TEAM FIRST AID KIT

- ▲ Butterfly bandages
- ▲ Antibiotic cream/ointment packets
- ▲ Electrolyte replacement (tablets, Emer'gen-C)
- ▲ Bandages (3 x 4 inches)
- ▲ Gauze roll (2 inches x 5 feet)
- ▲ Athletic tape
- ▲ Gauze pads (3 x 4 inches)
- ▲ Eye pads
- ▲ 1-inch-wide bandages

MountainQuest does not require personal first-aid kits. Each competitor is responsible for carrying what they need. The team first-aid kit must be carried at all times and must be capable of supporting three team members.

PERSONAL MANDATORY EQUIPMENT (TO BE CARRIED THROUGHOUT THE RACE)

- ▲ 1 headlamp
- ▲ 1 emergency blanket or bag
- ▲ 1 whistle
- ▲ 1 hat (for warmth)
- ▲ 1 hydration system (bottle or bladder)
- ▲ 1 polar fleece top
- ▲ 1 water/wind resistant jacket

PADDLE SECTION PERSONAL EQUIPMENT (IN ADDITION TO FULL-TIME MANDATORY GEAR)

- ▲ 1 Coast Guard–approved personal floatation device

MOUNTAIN BIKING PERSONAL EQUIPMENT (IN ADDITION TO FULL-TIME MANDATORY GEAR)

▲ 1 front-mounted bike light

▲ 1 rear-mounted flashing light

▲ 1 biking helmet

CLIMBING PERSONAL EQUIPMENT (IN ADDITION TO FULL-TIME MANDATORY GEAR)

▲ 1 climbing harness

▲ 2 locking carabiners

▲ 1 descending device

▲ 1 helmet (bike helmet is ok)

▲ 1 prusik

SALOMON X-ADVENTURE 2000

SAGA D'AVENTURES AND MOUNTAINQUEST ADVENTURES (NORTH AMERICAN STAGE)

ARTICLE VII— EQUIPMENT

1. **Racing Gear:** Competitors from the same team are asked to race wearing similar clothing, and with the racing number always clearly visible, including on life jackets.

2. **Compulsory Material:** The road-book (race instructions) will contain the compulsory material required for each section. Such equipment may be checked at any time. A team will not be allowed to set off if this equipment is not complete.

PER TEAM

▲ 1 compass or watch compass

▲ 1 altimeter or watch altimeter

▲ 1 whistle

▲ 1 knife with a foldable blade of minimum 15 centimeters (blade unfolded)

- ▲ 1 waterproof map holder
- ▲ Iodine or other water purification system
- ▲ Camping equipment: 1 tent for a minimum of two people, or 1 bivy bag per person (tents must be self-supporting, with no canvas to suspend; waterproof, roof and floor in one piece; and big enough to hold two people lying down)

PER RACER

- ▲ 1 headlamp (functioning)
- ▲ 1 survival blanket (minimum 2 x 1.5 meters)
- ▲ 1 flask capable of holding 1 liter (or bladder system)
- ▲ 1 harness
- ▲ 2 screw-locking carabiners
- ▲ 1 descender (type Figure 8)
- ▲ 1 one-piece wetsuit with full legs
- ▲ 1 mountain bike
- ▲ 1 mountain bike helmet
- ▲ Mountain bike lights (self-containing) front and rear, only material designed for bikes will be accepted
- ▲ 1 pair inline skates
- ▲ 1 life jacket U.S. Coast Guard–approved for kayaking (Type III)
- ▲ 1 headband or 1 hat
- ▲ 1 pair of long Lycra tights or long trousers
- ▲ 1 polar fur, minimum weight 250 grams (+/– 10 percent) without accessories, and independent from any type of wind cheater
- ▲ 1 waterproof mountain-type jacket, minimum weight 500 grams (+/– 10 percent without accessories, and independent from any type of polar fur)
- ▲ 1 pair of waterproof pants
- ▲ 1 backpack per person of (minimum of 18 liters), big enough to contain the compulsory material on all sections (night and day)

Each team member should carry their own compulsory material in their backpack. A small hydration backpack, such as a "CamelBak," may not replace a backpack.

ECO-CHALLENGE 2000

MANDATORY SAFETY EQUIPMENT LIST

Note: this is a listing of personal and team mandatory safety gear and first-aid kit requirements for the Eco-Challenge 2000 in Sabah, Borneo. Mandatory equipment for each of the disciplines is not given in this appendix.

PERSONAL MANDATORY SAFETY EQUIPMENT

Each competitor must carry the following equipment at all times during the race and must be prepared to present it to race organizers at any time for a mandatory gear check on the race course. This is to ensure each competitor's safety.

- ▲ 1 emergency strobe light (must be a proper emergency strobe, approximately 1 x 4 inches, flashing bike lights not accepted)
- ▲ 1 headlamp
- ▲ 1 survival mirror
- ▲ 1 survival blanket (space blanket)
- ▲ 1 compass
- ▲ 1 lighter
- ▲ 1 knife
- ▲ 1 whistle
- ▲ 1 smoke signal (to be distributed at race registration)
- ▲ 1 personal first-aid kit

PERSONAL MANDATORY FIRST-AID KIT

Each competitor must carry the following first-aid kit at all times and must be prepared to present it to race organizers at any time for a mandatory gear check on the race course. This is to ensure each competitor's safety.

- ▲ 1 valid credit card, $500 cash, or travelers' checks
- ▲ 10 blister dressings sufficient for ten race days (moleskin/Compeed)
- ▲ 1 roll of stretch gauze bandage material (3 inches x 5 feet)
- ▲ 1 roll of nonstretch Sports Strapping tape (not duct tape) (3 inches x 5 feet)
- ▲ 1 nonadherent wound dressing (2 x 3 inches)
- ▲ 1 pressure dressing for heavy bleeding (Combine pad) (3 x 5 inches)
- ▲ 100 milliliters broad-spectrum, waterproof sunscreen (SPF 15+)

- ▲ 100 tablets or 20 milliliters water purification tablets or liquid suitable for 100 liters
- ▲ 1 lip sunscreen
- ▲ 1 box waterproof matches
- ▲ 10 milliliters antiseptic solution (Betadine or iodine)
- ▲ 10 grams antibacterial ointment (Neosporin)
- ▲ 10 electrolyte replacement tablets or sachets, minimum sodium content 400 milligrams each
- ▲ 1 box waterproof matches
- ▲ 10 antidiarrheal medications (Lomotil or Imodium)
- ▲ 10 antihistamine tables (Claritin)
- ▲ 10 grams or 50 milliliters anti-itch spray, gel, or tablets (Eurax, Calagel)
- ▲ 10 grams, 50 milliliters, or 10 tablets anti-inflammatory spray, gel, or tablets (Advil, Tylenol, aspirin, paracetamol, ibuprofen)
- ▲ For those with known medical conditions, appropriate quantities of your required medications

TEAM MANDATORY SAFETY EQUIPMENT

Each team must carry the following equipment at all times during the race (these items may be divided up and carried by any team members). Teams must be prepared to present to race organizers at any time for a mandatory gear check on the racecourse. This is to ensure each competitor's safety.

- ▲ 2 aerial distress flares (to be distributed at race registration)
- ▲ 1 team first-aid kit
- ▲ 1 sealed emergency radio (provided by Eco-Challenge)
- ▲ 1 sealed emergency GPS (provided by Eco-Challenge)
- ▲ 1 altimeter
- ▲ Maps (provided by Eco-Challenge)

TEAM MANDATORY FIRST-AID KIT

Each team must carry the following equipment at all times during the race (these items may be divided up and carried by any team members). Teams must be prepared to present it to race organizers at any time for a mandatory gear check on the racecourse. This is to ensure each competitor's safety.

- ▲ 2 rolls of stretch gauze bandages (crepe or Ace wrap) (3 x 5 inches)

- ▲ 2 rolls of nonstretch Sports Strapping tape (not duct tape) (3 x 5 inches)
- ▲ 2 nonadherent wound dressings (2 x 3 inches)
- ▲ 2 pressure dressings for heavy bleeding (Combine pad) (3 x 5 inches)
- ▲ 1 pair of scissors
- ▲ 1 pair of tweezers

MANDATORY GEAR LIST FOR THE RAID GAULOISES 2000 TRANS-HIMALYAN (TIBET/NEPAL)

ARTICLE VI–EQUIPMENT

EQUIPMENT PROVIDED BY THE ORGANIZATION

- ▲ A set of maps for each team
- ▲ 2 Raid instruction books for each team
- ▲ 1 distress beacon for each team
- ▲ 6 flares
- ▲ Rafts, canoes, and swimming floats for each team
- ▲ 1 wooden crate (135 x 114 x 75 feet) for transporting the team's 5 bicycles

A deposit (check, credit card, or cash) is required for the loan of the distress beacon and flares. These deposits will be refunded when the equipment is returned in good condition at the end of the event. The beacons and flares are not covered by the insurance policies taken out by the organization.

REQUIRED EQUIPMENT

INDIVIDUAL EQUIPMENT

Throughout the race all competitors must have with them (the standard list):

- ▲ 1 survival blanket
- ▲ 1 case of 6 flares supplied by the organization
- ▲ 1 compass

- ▲ 1 whistle
- ▲ 1 head lamp
- ▲ 1 lighter
- ▲ 1 pair of sunglasses providing 100 percent UV and IR protection

TEAM EQUIPMENT

Throughout the race each team must have (the standard team list):

- ▲ 1 first-aid kit
- ▲ 2 altimeters (6,000 meters)
- ▲ A survival/signal mirror
- ▲ 2 knives designed for cutting ropes or straps (with sheath for nonfolding knives)
- ▲ 10 meters of climbing rope, minimum diameter 5 millimeters
- ▲ 1 distress beacon supplied by the organization
- ▲ 2 manually operated strobe lights (waterproof, 8 hours minimum stand-alone capacity)
- ▲ 1 spare pair of sunglasses providing 100 percent UV and IR protection

SUPPORT TEAM

- ▲ 1 first-aid kit
- ▲ Sufficient quantity of garbage bags to hold the team's refuse
- ▲ 1 metal shovel
- ▲ 1 tent or shelter to withstand extreme weather conditions
- ▲ Stove and pan to heat enough hot water for seven people
- ▲ Sufficient ropes for stowing all the equipment on the support vehicle
- ▲ 2 large heavy canvas bags, 100-to-150-liter capacity, bearing the team number
- ▲ 5 soft covers for the team bicycles
- ▲ Adequate clothing for the environment
- ▲ Trunks and other packing equipment to be transported by the organization to the starting point; maximum size: 2 trunks, 120 x 60 x 40 (60 kilograms); and 2 trunks, 100 x 55 x 40 (60 kilograms)

REQUIRED EQUIPMENT FOR HORSEBACK

For each team:

▲ Sufficient quantity of straps or ropes for securing the load on the horse

REQUIRED EQUIPMENT FOR MOUNTAIN BIKING

For each individual:

▲ 1 mountain bike with front suspension

▲ 1 helmet

▲ 1 pair of protective gloves with fingers

▲ 1 rear reflector attached to bike

▲ 1 front lamp attached to bike

For each team:

▲ 2 pumps

▲ 1 repair kit with sufficient quantity of repair materials for fixing flat tires, 1 chain repairer, and 2 odometers/speedometers

REQUIRED EQUIPMENT FOR CANYONEERING

For each individual:

▲ 1 climbing harness

▲ 1 Figure-8 type descender (other types not allowed)

▲ 1 rope with a figure-8 knot at each end (2.5 meters of dynamic rope, minimum diameter of 10 millimeters)

▲ 1 pair of suitable shoes

▲ 3 automatic locking carabiners

▲ 1 helmet

▲ 1 neoprene wetsuit

For each team:

▲ Minimum 1 backpack per team

▲ Sufficient quantity of waterproof bags for packing personal effects

REQUIRED EQUIPMENT FOR TREKKING

For each individual:

▲   1 telescopic walking stick (nontelescopic poles are not allowed)

REQUIRED EQUIPMENT FOR RAFTING AND CANOEING

For each individual:

▲   1 lifejacket (minimum of 140 Newtons for people weighing more than 60 kilograms, 110 Newtons for people weighing less than 60 kilograms)

▲   1 whitewater sports helmet

▲   1 pair of shoes

▲   1 thermal long-sleeved shirt and ankle-length pants

▲   1 neoprene wetsuit, minimum thickness 3 millimeters

▲   1 semi-waterproof nautical windbreaker

For each team:

▲   2 safety throw ropes (20 meters minimum)

▲   2 waterproof containers (cans of 5 liters minimum and 7 liters maximum capacity)

▲   Sufficient quantity of waterproof bags for packing personal effects

▲   2 raft (divers) knives to be fastened to the lifejacket

▲   2 bailing scoops

REQUIRED EQUIPMENT FOR WHITEWATER SWIMMING

For each individual:

▲   1 long johns–style wetsuit (minimum 3 millimeters thick)

▲   1 life jacket (minimum of 140 Newtons for people weighing more than 60 kilograms, 110 Newtons for people weighing less than 60 kilograms)

▲   1 whitewater sports helmet

▲   1 pair of fins/flippers (maximum length 33 centimeters—curved flippers not allowed)

▲   Leash attached to fins and competitor

▲   1 thermal long-sleeved shirt and ankle-length pants

- ▲ 1 semi-waterproof nautical windbreaker
- ▲ 1 pair of lightweight shoes or sandals with Velcro fastening
- ▲ Padding under wetsuit (shins, kneepads, thigh guards)

For each team:
- ▲ 2 safety throw ropes (20 meters minimum)
- ▲ 3 waterproof dry bags (10 liters minimum and 15 liters maximum capacity)
- ▲ 2 raft (divers) knives to be fastened to the life jacket

REQUIRED EQUIPMENT FOR TIBET

For each individual:
- ▲ 1 Gore-Tex–style jacket with hood
- ▲ 1 synthetic fleece top with sleeves (200 weight)
- ▲ 1 Gore-Tex–type pants
- ▲ 1 warm hat
- ▲ 1 pair of warm gloves

For the team:
- ▲ 1 stove, fuel, and pan
- ▲ 1 or 2 tents to fit team sitting or lying down (minimum total weight of 2.5 kilograms)
- ▲ Sleeping bag(s) for protection equivalent to –5°C

REQUIRED EQUIPMENT FOR NEPAL

For the team:
- ▲ A lightweight tarpaulin, made of waterproof fabric or woven canvas

MANDATORY FIRST-AID KIT FOR EACH TEAM

Medicinal drugs:
- ▲ Mild pain and fever (aspirin, ibuprofen in sufficient quantity)
- ▲ Level II antalgic (combination of paracetamol-dextropropoxyphenum or codeine)
- ▲ Antispasmodic (Phlorogucinol)

- ▲ Simple intestinal remedy (Smecta)
- ▲ Gastric remedy (Maalox)
- ▲ Antidiarrheal (Imodium)
- ▲ Antiemetic (Metoclopramide, Primperan tablets)
- ▲ Nonsteroidal anti-inflammatory (Diclofenac)
- ▲ Muscle relaxant (Flexeril)
- ▲ Asthma attack inhaler (Salbutamol aerosol)
- ▲ Anti-UV protective eye drops (Uveline)
- ▲ Antiseptic eye drops (Biocidan)
- ▲ Personal medications

Bandages for wound care:
- ▲ 1 pair of tweezers
- ▲ 1 pair of fine scissors
- ▲ 1 or 2 hypodermic needles for piercing blisters
- ▲ Sterile compresses (40 x 40 millimeters)
- ▲ Antiseptic (Chlorhexidine, iodine)
- ▲ Drying solution (Eosine)
- ▲ Self-adhesive bandages (Coban wrap)
- ▲ Adhesive bandages for strapping and setting, such as Ace bandages
- ▲ Blister protection products (Compeed, Moleskin)
- ▲ Moisturizing ointment for burns
- ▲ Sunscreen—15 SPF minimum
- ▲ Epitasis, or dental bleeding stick
- ▲ 1 survival blanket

APPENDIX B

TOP ADVENTURE RACERS' TRAINING WORKOUTS

© 2000 Salomon N.A./Thomas Zuccareno

There are a lot of similarities in the training done by many of the top adventure racers in the world. It is interesting to note that the typical training week for even some of the best adventure racers does not usually include more than fifteen to twenty hours—certainly encouraging for everyone trying to fit their workout into an already crowded schedule. Almost everyone includes some kind of strength training, whether it is in the gym or outside. Harald Zundel, whose team took first place at the FogDog 24-Hour Adventure Race 2000, likes to incorporate one or two outdoor strength sessions into his weekly schedule. These include mostly Navy SEAL calisthenics such as push-ups, pull-ups, and abdominal exercises, and stairs to strengthen the legs.

Adventure racer Rebecca Rusch maintains her strength in much the same way, without the use of a gym, by including sit-ups, push-ups, and pull-ups into her training on a semi-regular basis. Other top adventure racers, including Mike Kloser—winner of the Eco-Challenge 2000—believe we naturally incorporate strength training by doing physical labor, including construction projects and working on volunteer trail projects. Swedish racer Mats Anderson of Team Salomon Human Link and top U.S. adventure racer Ian Adamson include a whole body weight-training regimen one day per week, whereas another racer, Robyn Benincasa, prefers to lift weights about ten times per month, focusing on her upper body.

Petri Forsman, whose accomplishments with Team Nokia include winning the Raid Gauloises 2000, the Mild Seven Outdoor Quest 2000, and the Extreme Sports Mexican Championship 2000, includes a strength/power training session two times each week for his upper body during the winter months. For the legs, his strength training includes a pyramid training set with free weights that takes him about forty-five minutes to complete. The importance of including hills in the training schedule for strength was emphasized by nearly everyone. Uniquely, in the winter Petri includes hill repeats and intervals, both running and biking, by training in a mine—because of the large amount of snow Finland often has. The climb in the mine is 320 meters, repeated two to three times for running and two to six times for biking.

Almost all of these competitors do the majority of their bike training on their mountain bikes. Adventure racer Terho Lahtinen of Team K2 summarized what many competitors indicated when he stated that "mountain biking is much more interesting and versatile training than road bike riding." The exceptions to this thought include Robyn and Antonio de la Rosa of Team RedBull PlayStation from Spain, whose road bike training represents about 75 percent of the overall bike training.

One of the most notable differences between training schedules in the United States and those in Europe is the inclusion of orienteering as a standard part of the typical training week. Petri, Mats, Terho, and Antonio all say that running orienteering races and training in navigation are important parts of their training.

Cross-training plays an important role in overall training for all adventure racers, according to each of these competitors. Ian, Mats, Mike, Petri, and Rebecca all like to Nordic ski in the winter, while Paul Romero of Team Epinephren snowboards frequently. Many of these adventure racers also train by inline skating, playing soccer, and swimming. Harald is a proponent of including yoga regularly in his training schedule.

When should you take a break from training? Petri and Ian simply take a day off when they feel tired; others, like Antonio and Rebecca, incorporate one day off per week into their training schedules. Many racers indicated that having a scheduled day off helps make time to spend with family and friends, take care of business, and as the fun-loving Antonio says, drink beer, take saunas and Jacuzzis, and chase women.

What follows are descriptions of typical training plans for these top adventure racers, beginning with the more structured training regimes and ending with mostly intuitive or free-form training plans. They are reflective of training plans roughly two months before a major race.

IAN ADAMSON, USA
Eco-Challenge (2000 1st, 1997 1st, 1996 1st)
ELF Authentic Adventure Race 1999 (2nd)
Southern Traverse Adventure Race (1998 2nd, 1996 1st)
ESPN X-Games (1997 1st, 1996 2nd)
Mild Seven Outdoor Quest (1999 2nd, 1997 2nd)
Raid Gauloises (1998 1st)

Given ideal conditions and race calendar, Ian likes to peak about two weeks prior to a big race. This allows him plenty of time to taper without losing condition.

In general, for peak performance in a big race, he needs at least a one-month recovery from the previous event, but this can vary up to six months if his last race was particularly demanding, as was the case with the ELF Authentic Adventure Race 1999 and Raid Gauloises 1998.

A typical peak workout week for Ian would be:

Monday	Smooth trail run or high altitude hike (14,000-foot peak) (4 to 8 hours)
Tuesday	Paddle intervals (1 hour), rock climbing (1 hour)
Wednesday	Mountain bike ride on varied terrain (4 hours)
Thursday	Run intervals or fartlek (1 hour), white water paddle (1 hour)
Friday	Paddle, open water (4 hours)
Saturday	Road bike intervals/hills (1 hour), weights (40 to 60 minutes)
Sunday	Cross training, usually social Nordic/backcountry skiing, snowshoeing, inline skating or swimming (varies from 1 to 6 hours)

Ian aims to cover long endurance, intensity (hills, intervals), and skills (white water, trails, technical mountain biking, etc.) in each of the core sports of running, biking, paddling, and climbing as well as any disciplines specific to the next event. He trains in all types of weather, and as he puts it, "especially the ugly stuff since these are likely race conditions."

Since Ian feels weights can be useful for muscular balance and to improve general strength, he does one set each to failure exercises replicating paddle, bike, run, climb, skate, etc. He tries to eliminate rest between exercises, so he can maintain an elevated heart rate and supplement cardiovascular conditioning.

Because rest is extremely important to facilitate recovery and repair, Ian incorporates rest with sleep, taking midday naps if practical and days off, depending on how he feels. He notes that taking anywhere up to a week of rest will not harm your fitness, and may provide a necessary mental break from heavy training. Also, he avoids sleep deprivation and extremely long sessions at high intensity unless he is training for a short event, like the Mild Seven Outdoor Quest or Salomon X-Adventure Race.

Lastly, Ian does map and compass work setting adventure racing courses for his navigation training.

PETRI FORSMAN, FINLAND

Raid Gauloises 2000 (1st)
Mild Seven Outdoor Quest 2000 (1st)
Extreme Sports Mexican Championship 2000 (1st)

Monday	Paddle (kayak) (2 hours), run (2 hours, evening)
Tuesday	Mountain bike ride (1.75 hours), orienteering high intensity (50 minutes, evening)
Wednesday	Run (1.25 hours), mountain bike, technical (1.75 hours, evening)
Thursday	Paddle (kayak) (1 hour 10 minutes with eight 2-minute intervals), run (45 minutes, evening)
Friday	Run (45 minutes)
Saturday	Adventure race, if possible (8 to 10 hours)
Sunday	Sail (4 hours), for fun

Plus: 1 to 2 hours of walking each day with his dog.

HARALD ZUNDEL, USA

FogDog 24-Hour Adventure Race 2000 (1st)

Mild Seven Outdoor Quest (2000 7th, 1999 4th)

Southern Traverse 1999 (7th)

Eco-Challenge 2000 (11th)

Monday	Run (45 minutes), paddle (2 hours), yoga (2 hours)
Tuesday	Run (1.25 hours), road bike ride (2.25 hours), paddle (1 hour)
Wednesday	Road bike ride (3 to 4 hours), paddle (1 hour)
Thursday	Run (1.25 hours), mountain bike (1 hour, 20 minutes)
Friday	Strength/Speed workout (1 to 2 hours), paddle (2 hours)
Saturday	Road bike ride (5 to 6 hours), run (45 minutes)
Sunday	Mountain bike (2 to 3 hours), paddle (1 to 2 hours), inline skate (1 to 2 hours)

TERHO LAHTINEN, FINLAND

Mild Seven Outdoor Quest (2000 3rd, 1998 1st)

Raid Gauloises 2000 (12th)

Salomon X-Adventure 1998 (Norway 1st, Finland 1st, Spain 2nd)

Monday	Easy, recovery from weekend training: run (40 minutes) or inline skate (1 hour); massage
Tuesday	Orienteering (1.25 to 1.50 hours, fast) or interval run (70 to 80 minutes with five 4-minute intervals with 2 minutes recovery)
Wednesday	Trail run (2 hours) or mountain bike (2 to 3 hours) or a combination of run (1 hour) and mountain bike (1.5 hours)
Thursday	Strength training with 15 minutes of running before and after
Friday	Run (1 hour, or 30 minutes if doing an orienteering race on Saturday)
Saturday	Run (70 to 90 minutes, with 35 to 60 minutes very fast), kayak (1 to 1.5 hours) or orienteering race
Sunday	Combination training (4 to 7 hours) including mountain biking, kayaking, and running

MICHAEL KLOSER, USA

Eco-Challenge (2000 1st, 1998 1st)

Mild Seven Outdoor Quest 2000 (2nd)

World Mountain Bike Champion 1988

Monday	Run (20 minutes)
Tuesday	Mountain bike (2 hours)
Wednesday	Run (30 minutes to 1 hour), mountain bike (1 to 1.5 hours)
Thursday	Paddle (1 to 2 hours)
Friday	Recovery day
Saturday	Mountain bike (2 to 4 hours), whitewater or flat water paddle (1 to 2 hours)
Sunday	Climb, hike, or ski up a 12,000-to-14,000-foot peak or two and ski down in winter

ANTONIO DE LA ROSA, SPAIN

Eco-Challenge (1999 2nd, 1998 3rd)

Mild Seven Outdoor Quest (1999 3rd, 1997 3rd)

Salomon X-Adventure 1999 (Spain 1st, Japan 1st)

Extreme Sports Mexican Championship (2000 2nd, 1999 1st)

Monday	Road bike (3 hours, morning), run (1 hour, afternoon)
Tuesday	Mountain trek (3 to 4 hours), paddle (kayak) (1.5 hours)
Wednesday	Mountain bike ride (3.5 hours), swim (3,000 meters)
Thursday	Run (1.25 hours), paddle (kayak) (1.25 hours)
Friday	Relax and party all night (good sleep deprivation training)
Saturday	Road ride (4 hours), run (50 minutes)
Sunday	Road bike (2.5 hours), paddle (kayak) (2 hours)

MATS ANDERSON, SWEDEN

Salomon X-Adventure 1999

(Sweden 1st, Spain 3rd, Scotland 2nd, Japan 2nd)

Raid Gauloises (1995 11th, 1997 7th)

Eco-Challenge 1997 (10th)

Mild Seven Outdoor Quest (1998 7th, 1999 9th)

Monday	Run (2 hours)
Tuesday	Paddle (1.5 hours)
Wednesday	Mountain bike ride (2 hours)
Thursday	Rest day
Friday	Run (1 hour), mountain bike (1 hour)
Saturday	Paddle (2 hours), mountain bike (2 hours)
Sunday	Trail run with a backpack (4 hours)

ROBYN BENINCASA, USA

Raid Gauloises (2000 4th, 1999 1st)

Eco-Challenge (2000 1st, 1999 4th, 1995 2nd)

Southern Traverse 2000 (3rd)

Raid the North Extreme 1998 (1st)

Robyn's work schedule doesn't allow her to follow a day-by-day training program. In general her workout week includes:

Paddle (kayak):	2 to 3 times per week with a local junior Olympic team
Road bike ride:	100 to 120 miles week
Mountain bike ride:	1 time per week
Run:	5 times per week for 50 to 70 miles, with one interval workout

REBECCA RUSCH, USA

Eco-Challenge (2000 8th, 1999 4th)
Raid Gauloises 2000 (7th)

Rebecca also claims not to have a typical training week. She does not preplan her training but follows her heart, head, and body, and tailors her training to the upcoming race.

PAUL ROMERO, USA

Hi-Tec Adventure Racing Series (15 consecutive top 3 finishes)
ELF Authentic Adventure Race 1999 (2nd)
Expedition Mata Atlantica 2000 (1st)
Cal-Eco Race Series 2000 (1st)

Paul races as much as possible during the year, lots of short (2-to-24-hour) races that don't leave much time for training. He focuses on tailoring his training and training conditions to the upcoming race, and he runs, paddles, and bikes daily.

APPENDIX C

BEING A RACE VOLUNTEER

© 1998 Dan Campbell

One of the best ways to learn about adventure racing in preparation for your first race is to volunteer to staff a race. Race directors depend on hardworking, dedicated volunteers to ensure a successful race. Volunteers are needed to:

- ▲ Help with team check in and gear check.
- ▲ Staff checkpoints on the course.
- ▲ Manage transition areas.
- ▲ Transport food/water around the course for other volunteers.
- ▲ Help with loading and transport of gear (unsupported races).
- ▲ Oversee radio/cell phone communications, battery charging, equipment checkout.
- ▲ Inflate boats (and patch if necessary).
- ▲ Set up start/finish line and sponsor banners.
- ▲ Obtain items from town, copy maps and race instructions (in other words, be a gofer).
- ▲ Provide medical assistance if you are trained and certified.
- ▲ Provide a "sweep" of the course after the final teams go through a checkpoint.
- ▲ Assist with tear-down and cleanup of TAs and finish area after the race.
- ▲ Assist with computer/results compilation.

The course director and/or volunteer coordinator will provide you with information about the race prior to the event. They will let you know what is needed and what tasks you will be doing so you will be prepared. If race management has a volunteer meeting to learn about what you will be doing and to view the course prior to the race, take advantage of it. The more you know about the course and the location of the checkpoints, the more valuable you will be once the race has started.

Volunteers will be given instructions and maps. Study the maps that are provided to you before the race. If you are responsible for setting up a checkpoint, know exactly where it is supposed to be. If you own a global positioning system and know how to use it, be sure to bring it along so that you will be able to verify the Universal Transverse Mercator coordinates and make sure you are where you are supposed to be.

Ideally, the race director would like to have a group of volunteers who can commit to helping during the entire race. If you cannot do that, then let them know what kind of a commitment you can make. The race coordinator needs to know your availability to determine where and when to use your help. It will also help them ensure they have the appropriate number of people scheduled to cover the event. If you have volunteered to help, please honor your commitment to the best of your ability—the racers are relying on you.

Volunteers at the checkpoints and TAs areas spend a lot of their time waiting for teams, possibly in bad weather. You must be prepared with appropriate clothing and camping gear if that is what is required of you. Look over the list of suggested items for support crews to carry (see page 50) to get an idea of the items you should have with you. Ask the race management for a list of the required gear the racers must have. Always have the personal emergency equipment, such as a whistle, emergency mirror, compass, and waterproof matches with you during the race. You will most likely be provided with a radio to communicate information from your location and for your use in an emergency. If you have volunteered to be out on the course during the race, you must be prepared to be self-sufficient for long periods of time. This means having adequate food, water, clothing, and shelter.

ADDED BENEFITS

Volunteers manning one of the checkpoints in the mountains during the Salomon X-Adventure Race 2000 in Aspen, Colorado, had a surprise visit from one of the area locals who had a mountain residence nearby. Realizing that the volunteers were probably in for a long night and would enjoy some good food, actor Don Johnson, of *Miami Vice* fame, treated the volunteers to steak and other great food and drink.

Volunteering at a race can be an exciting and gratifying way to learn about adventure racing. You will meet racers and other volunteers like you; who knows—you might even find teammates to race with in the future. You will take home at least a T-shirt for your effort and many great memories, along with the excitement to form your own team and race next time!

Some race organizations to contact online are:

MountainQuest Adventures: www.mountain-quest.com

Odyssey Adventures: www.beastoftheeast.com

California Sport Marketing: www.csmevents.com

Frontier Adventure Racing (Raid the North):
www.raidthenorth.com

Michael Epstein Sports Productions (Hi-Tec Racing Series and FogDog 24-Hour Adventure Race): www.mesp.com

Four Winds Adventure Races: www.4windsadventure.com

Eco-Challenge Productions: www.eco-challenge.com

Adventurous Concepts: www.FloridaRaces.com

Terra Firma Adventure Races: www.terrafirmapromo.com

GLOSSARY OF ADVENTURE LANGUAGE

Any new sport brings with it a unique language. Adventure racing is no different and has its share of terms that both borrow from other activities or are totally new. Below is a listing of the common terms and abbreviations encountered in an adventure race, and their meaning.

Abseil. A rappel down a cliff face using approved harness and a descending device such as an ATC (see *ATC)* or Figure 8.

ATC. Originally the Black Diamond Air Traffic Controller belay device that can be used for rappelling, now commonly refers to any of the tubular-style of rappel or belay devices.

Bailer. Scoop used to remove water from a boat.

Bladder. A water reservoir or hydration system usually made of vinyl plastic, with a tube long enough to go from the reservoir to the mouth. The tube has a bite valve on it that allows the wearer to bite and suck on the end of the tube to drink water when needed.

Brake hand. The dominant hand used by a rappeller *(see* Figure 8)to control the descent on a fixed rope.

Canadian canoe. Term used outside of the United States to refer to open canoes and canoeing versus *canoe*, which can refer to canoes and kayaks.

Canyoneering/Canyoning. Sport involving travel on foot following the course of a river or stream through a canyon. Usually involves the use of ropes to rappel down waterfalls or steep cliffs. *Canyoning* is the term used outside of the United States.

Carabiners, or biners. Metal snap-links used to attach the descending device or ascending device to a climbing harness, or used to clip into a fixed safety line to traverse a section.

Checkpoint (CP). Also called passport control (PC). Race-management location where the team passport is marked with the time and location. All teams must go through each checkpoint.

Class I-VI water. International classification of moving water, with Class I water the easiest to navigate and Class VI difficult even for experienced boaters.

Coasteering. The sport of traveling by foot along the coast of a water body, such as the ocean or a lake.

Crampons. Device worn on the foot over the boot or shoe to provide additional grip and support when traveling on snow, ice, and glaciers.

Cutoff. Specific time of day at a designated location in the race where competitors reaching the location after the posted time will not be allowed to continue the race.

Daisy chain. See *sling/daisy chain.*

Dark zone. An area where teams are not allowed to proceed after dark, due to safety considerations.

Dead fall. Refers to trees and other dead material that cover the forest floor and may make traveling through a forested area very difficult and slow.

Dry bag. A sealable bag made of waterproof material that can be used to keep gear and clothing dry during water sections of the adventure race.

Duct tape. Shiny silver tape that no adventure racer should be without. It sticks to itself and can be used for numerous purposes, such as to prevent blisters by eliminating friction spots or to hold broken gear together. Usually carried by wrapping around a water bottle, trekking pole, or other item that competitors are carrying anyway.

Expedition-style race. Long race where competitors are required to carry large amounts of gear and food with them throughout the race. Can be supported or unsupported.

Figure 8. A metal descending device (shaped like a figure 8) that is used to perform a rappel. It is attached to the rappeller's climbing harness and the main rope.

Foot Fungus. A common infection among adventure racers brought on when the competitor's feet remain wet for long periods of time.

Gaiters. Short or long leg coverings worn when trekking or during snow travel. They seal the area between the leg or pant and shoe, covering the cuff of the shoe and keeping the legs from getting scratched by vegetation or wet from snow, and keeping small pebbles and dirt out of the shoe.

Gear check. Event prior to the start of the adventure race where race management observes that each team has the appropriate and required gear for the race.

Gear drop. Location where the support crew has left gear for the next event.

Global positioning system (GPS). An electronic system for determining the user's location using satellites. Although usually not allowed in adventure races, they can be provided by race management to be used in emergency situations.

Halogen bulb. A very bright light source that can be put into a headlamp or bike light. Although they are bright, the burn time is generally short (less than four hours).

Hike-a-bike. An unrideable section of the bike course due to rocks or dead fall across the trail, excessive mud, or steepness of the trail. Competitors usually walk their bikes through these sections.

Jumar. Refers to ascending a fixed rope using a Jumar or other brand of ascending device.

Kayak skirt. See *spray skirt*.

K2–K4. Description of the number of people that a kayak is designed for. For example a K2 is a kayak that holds two people who are paddling.

LED lamp. A headlamp that contains LED lights that will burn for long periods of time (up to 100-plus hours) and provide a diffuse type of light.

Leptospirosis. A bacterial infection picked up from floodwaters containing contaminated animal urine and feces. Competitors in the Eco-Challenge 2000 in Borneo became ill after getting infected.

Lithium batteries. A more expensive type of battery with higher performance; longer lasting than alkaline batteries.

Mandatory gear. A list of required equipment and clothing, typically required to complete the event and provide safety in an accident or during changing weather.

Meal Ready-to Eat (MRE). A high-calorie packaged military food substance popular in long adventure races.

Mystery events. Events included in some adventure races (popular in the Hi-Tec races). They are unannounced events that can occur at any stage of the race and often involve team-building tasks such as greased wall climbs and log carries.

Navigation. (1) To find one's way from checkpoint to checkpoint; usually involves the use of a map and compass. Sometimes referred to as "orienteering." (2) Travel on water, boating (typical usage outside of the United States).

Orienteering. See *navigation*.

Passport. Small book that must be carried with the team at all times to mark their progress through the race. Loss of the passport results in a time penalty or disqualification.

Passport control (PC). See *checkpoint*.

Personal flotation device (PFD). A life jacket usually required for boating and swimming sections. Race management might specify a certain flotation requirement (pounds of flotation, class level of jacket, or Newtons of floatation).

Portage. Carrying a boat over land from one body of water to another, over a dam, or over a peninsula.

Prologue. An introductory or preceding event—occasionally taking place before the start of an expedition-length race to give competitors a chance to get used to a new sport, equipment, or altitude.

Prusik. Safety rope made of small diameter static cord and applied to the main rope and the competitor to create a friction knot as a safety backup on a rappel or other rope travel.

Puppy pile. Cozy sleeping arrangement for the team—to keep each other warm.

Rappel. Travel down a rock or other steep slope by means of a fixed rope and descending device such as a Figure 8.

Rogaine. A twenty-four-hour team orienteering race. Rogaine stands for "rugged outdoor group activity involving navigation and endurance."

Safety throw bag. A small bag containing a length of floating rope that can be thrown to someone in the water. The person throwing the bag holds on to one end; the person in the water grabs the thrown rope/bag and can be pulled to shore. Used in a river/swift water rescue.

Shortened course. Teams may be placed onto a shortened or alternate course due to weather or length of time it is taking teams to complete the race. The creation of a shortened course allows teams to continue to race, but in a separate division from those teams completing the entire, original racecourse.

Skills test. Event prior to the start of the adventure race where race management observes that each team and team member has the requisite skills required in the race and/or demonstrates the particular skills and methods used in the race to each competitor. The most common skills tested are river safety skills (ability to use a safety throw bag) and ropes skills.

Sleep deprivation. Condition that occurs during long races that continue through the nighttime. Effects are due to a lack of sleep and can include hallucinations, lack of judgment or coordination, and other symptoms.

Sling/daisy chain. Connectors made of webbing or rope that are connected to the climbing harness, ascenders, feet, or a combination of these.

Spray skirt. Also called kayak skirt. Neoprene or nylon material worn around the waist of the kayaker and attached over the combing of the kayak. The skirt keeps water from splashing into and filling the boat.

Sprint race. A two-to-four-hour adventure race composed of teams and usually involving mystery events. Example is the Hi-Tec race series.

Stage race. An adventure race that is staged over multiple days. Racing (and the clock) is halted at night and resumes in the morning. The team with the lowest total running time is declared the winner.

Support crew. Typically one or two persons who transport the competitors' gear from one transition point to the next, provide food at the transition area, help plan strategy and route finding, relay weather and race information, and generally assist with all aspects of preparation during the race.

Transition Area (TA). Checkpoint where your gear and support crew are located. Typically the transition area is the finish of one event (such as biking) and the beginning of a new one (such as paddling).

Team biathlon. Discipline similar to the "ride-and-tie" race format where, for example, a team of four has two bikes or two horses and the team leapfrogs forward by exchanging bikes (or horses) and running.

Towing system. Towing systems are devices attached from one person to another, one bike to another, or one boat to another, to assist in team travel by helping slower or ailing team members travel with the team.

Track. Jeep road or 4 × 4 dirt road, a term often used in races outside of the United States.

Trekking. Hiking over long distances with backpacks; an arduous journey or exploration. One of the core disciplines of adventure racing, it usually makes up one-third of the total race time.

Tyrolean traverse, or traverse. A rope skills event, with each team member traveling across a deep canyon or a river while clipped to the rope. Also known as highline, zip line, or flying fox.

Unranked. Teams become unranked when one team member must drop out of the race or they miss a race cutoff. The team is sometimes allowed to continue (minus one teammate) but they are no longer in the overall race ranking.

Universal Transverse Mercator (UTM). Mapping coordinate system that divides the world into a grid where grid lines are 1000 meters apart. UTM coordinates are frequently provided by race management to indicate the position of checkpoints and transition areas.

Wetsuit. A neoprene suit of varying lengths and styles designed to keep the wearer warm in water.

CREDITS AND CAPTIONS FOR COLOR SECTION

Page 1. Main photo: Traverse and ascent above the Colorado River, 1995 Eco-Challenge in Utah; © 1995 Dan Campbell. Inset photos: At the top of the 12,000-foot ascent; © 1995 Dan Campbell. Team Southern Traverse paddling on Lake Powell; © 1995 Dan Campbell.

Pages 2 and 3. Main photo: Out of the mist after a long night, 1997 Eco-Challenge in Australia; © 1997 Dan Campbell. Inset photos: Team Salomon Eco-Internet winning the 2000 Eco-Challenge in Borneo; © 2000 Dan Campbell. Rappelling through a thundering waterfall, 1999 Eco-Challenge in Argentina; © 1999 Dan Campbell.

Pages 4 and 5. Main Photo: Paddling Lake Powell during the final leg of the race, 1995 Eco-Challenge in Utah; © 1995 Dan Campbell. Inset photos: Navigating as a team; © 1995 Dan Campbell. Rappelling; © 1996 Dan Campbell. Ascending out of the Madai Caves, 2000 Eco-Challenge in Borneo; © 2000 Dan Campbell.

Pages 6 and 7. Main photo: The many faces of winter adventure, 2000 Salomon Winter Adventure Race in Colorado; © 2000 Phil Mislinski. Inset photos: The climb gets steeper, 1996 Eco-Challenge in British Columbia; © 1996 Dan Campbell. Winter running and biking, 2000 Salomon Winter Adventure Race in Colorado; © 2000 Phil Mislinski. Skiing, 2000 Salomon Winter Adventure Race in Colorado; © 2000 Phil Mislinski. Descending from the summit of Mount Tronador, 1999 Eco-Challenge in Argentina; © 1999 Dan Campbell.

Pages 8 and 9. Main photo: Navigating the coastline (coasteering) at high tide, 1998 Eco-Challenge in Morocco; © 1998 Dan Campbell. Inset photos: Tyrolean Traverse, 1999 MountainQuest "Race with an Altitude" in Colorado; © 1999 Darrin Eisman.

Pages 10 and 11. Main photo: Empty . . . nothing left to give, 2000 Eco-Challenge in Borneo; © 2000 Dan Campbell. Inset photos: Receiving a helping hand along the way, 2000 Salomon Winter Adventure Race in Colorado; © 2000 Phil Mislinski. Crossing a river on mountain bikes, 1997 Eco-Challenge in Australia; © 1997 Dan Campbell. Peddling the long hot road, 2000 Eco-Challenge in Borneo; © 2000 Mark S. Cosslett.

Pages 12 and 13. Main photo: A romp in the surf, 1996 Eco-Challenge in Australia; © 1996 Dan Campbell. Water break, 1997 Eco-Challenge in Utah; © 1997 Dan Campbell. Getting some stitches after being kicked by a horse, 1995 Eco-Challenge in Utah; © 1995 Dan Campbell. Taking a nap, 1997 Eco-Challenge in Australia; © 1997 Dan Campbell. We're going where? 1998 Eco-Challenge in Morocco; © 1998 Dan Campbell. Running, 2000 Salomon X-Adventure in Aspen, Colorado; © 2000 Salomon N.A./Thomas Zuccareno. Trekking through rocky terrain, 2000 Salomon X-Adventure in Aspen, Colorado; © 2000 Salomon N.A./Thomas Zuccareno.

Pages 14 and 15. Main photo: Team Vail crossing Lago Nahuel Huapi during the kayak leg of the 1999 Eco-Challenge in Argentina; © 1999 Dan Campbell. Crashing through the breakers, 1998 Eco-Challenge in Morocco; © 1998 Dan Campbell. Sea kayaking with a sail to harness the wind, 1997 Eco-Challenge in Australia; © 1997 Dan Campbell.

Page 16. Main photo: Ascending out of the Madai Caves, 2000 Eco-Challenge in Borneo; © 2000 Dan Campbell. Start of a 400-foot rappel, 1995 Eco-Challenge in Utah; © 1995 Dan Campbell. Traversing the gorge, 1999 MountainQuest "Race with an Altitude" in Colorado; © 1999 Darrin Eisman.

INDEX

© 2000 Phil Mislinski

ABOUT THE AUTHORS

© 2000 Dan Campbell

BARRY SIFF and **LIZ CALDWELL** are co-owners of MountainQuest Adventures. Both are experienced endurance athletes with competitive backgrounds in adventure racing that includes 11th place in the Eco-Challenge 2000 and 9th place in the Raid Gauloises 2000.

Barry was formerly the senior vice president of human resources for a multi-billion-dollar company. He is a contributing editor to *Inside Triathlon*. He lives with his wife, Judy, and son Elliot in Fort Collins, Colorado. His oldest son, Brian, is currently serving in the Peace Corps in Africa.

Liz is a Ph.D. environmental toxicologist and has operated her own environmental consulting company. She is an active member of Larimer County Search and Rescue and lives with her husband, Gary, and son, Skylar, in Fort Collins, Colorado.

Barry and Liz can be reached through their website: www.mountain-quest.com.